DRAGONS

DRAGONS

A Natural History

DR. KARL SHUKER

FOREWORD BY

DR. DESMOND MORRIS

EVERGREEN

EVERGREEN is an imprint of
TASCHEN GmbH

© 2006 TASCHEN GmbH
Hohenzollernring 53, D-50672 Köln
www.taschen.com

© 1995 by Marshall Editions
© Text 1995 Dr. Karl Shuker

Production this edition:
Textcase, Hilversum - The Netherlands

Printed in China

ISBN : 3-8228-5152-3

In loving memory of Gerald Durrell—
conservation's valorous St. George

CONTENTS

1 CANADA
Serpent dragons and serpent whales
2 U.S.A.
Serpent dragons and serpent whales
Kitchi-at'husis and the giant leech
The piasa
3 MEXICO
Quetzalcoatl
4 CHILE
The basilisk and the cockatrice
5 JAMAICA
The basilisk and the cockatrice
6 ICELAND
The basilisk and the cockatrice
7 IRELAND
Long-necks and sea lizards
8 GREAT BRITAIN
The Lambton worm
Serpent dragons and serpent whales
The Mordiford wyvern
The Wantley dragon
Amphipteres and winged serpents
Winged serpents of Wales
The basilisk and the cockatrice
Long-necks and sea lizards

9 SCANDINAVIA
Jormungander, the Midgard serpent
Serpent dragons and serpent whales
The Lindorm king
Fafnir
10 AUSTRIA, GERMANY, AND SWITZERLAND
The tatzelworm
The dragonet of Mount Pilatus
11 FRANCE
Guivres and gargouilles
The tarasque
The peluda
12 ITALY
The Carthaginian serpent giant
The tatzelworm
The salamander and the pyrallis
13 GREECE
The dragon of Poseidon
The Lernaean hydra
The salamander and the pyrallis

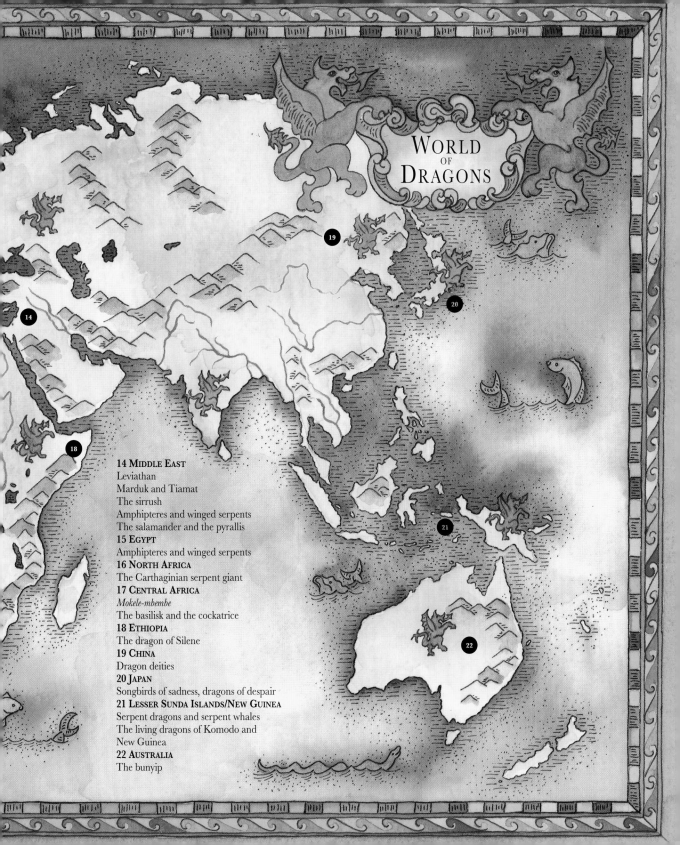

WORLD
OF
DRAGONS

14 MIDDLE EAST
Leviathan
Marduk and Tiamat
The sirrush
Amphipteres and winged serpents
The salamander and the pyrallis
15 EGYPT
Amphipteres and winged serpents
16 NORTH AFRICA
The Carthaginian serpent giant
17 CENTRAL AFRICA
Mokele-mbembe
The basilisk and the cockatrice
18 ETHIOPIA
The dragon of Silene
19 CHINA
Dragon deities
20 JAPAN
Songbirds of sadness, dragons of despair
21 LESSER SUNDA ISLANDS/NEW GUINEA
Serpent dragons and serpent whales
The living dragons of Komodo and
New Guinea
22 AUSTRALIA
The bunyip

FOREWORD

In the world of fantastic animals, the dragon is unique. No other imaginary creature has appeared in such a rich variety of forms. It is as though there was once a whole family of different dragon species that really existed, before they mysteriously became extinct. Indeed, as recently as the seventeenth century, scholars wrote of dragons as though they were scientific fact, their anatomy and natural history being recorded in painstaking detail.

The naturalist Edward Topsell, for instance, writing in 1608, considered them to be reptilian and closely related to serpents: "There are divers sorts of Dragons, distinguished partlie by their Countries, partlie by their quantitie and magnitude, and partlie by the different forme of their externall partes."

Unlike Shakespeare, who spoke of "the dragon more feared than seen," Topsell was convinced that they had been observed by many people: "Neither have we in Europe only heard of Dragons and never seen them, but also in our own country there have (by the testimony of sundry writers) divers been discovered and killed."

To be honest, it is rather disappointing that, when the natural world was thoroughly explored in the nineteenth century, no truly awe-inspiring dragons were brought to light. A few giant snakes and large lizards were unearthed as those amazing Victorian naturalists scoured the world for new specimens for their burgeoning

In this Russian icon (c.1600), St. George slays a wyvernlike dragon, whose tail bears four small heads.

collections, but not a single full-blooded, fire-breathing, wing-flapping dragon was captured, or even glimpsed in the distance.

From now on, the concept of the dragon would have to be tossed into the cauldron of fiction, to be gobbled up by cartoonists and animators, for cheap jokes and visual clichés. How much better it would have been if only some of them had turned out to be real living and breathing creatures that we could, at great risk and with enormous difficulty, encounter and marvel at today.

It was not to be, but, in memory at least, great dragons can still be treated with respect, as if they—like the mighty dinosaurs before them—once ruled the world, but have since fallen on hard times. This they deserve, if only to allow us to celebrate the imagination of the many early artists who so lovingly portrayed them over the centuries.

With this in mind, I had intended for many years to write a natural history of dragons. But now, perhaps, I do not need to bother because Karl Shuker has done it for me. I am immensely grateful to him, and I shall treasure the book he has compiled to take us into the wonderfully strange draconian world.

Desmond Morris

INTRODUCTION

Far away in the twilight time
Of every people, in every clime,
Dragons and griffins and monsters dire,
Born of water, and air, and fire,
Or nursed, like the Python, in the mud
And ooze of the old Deucalion flood,
Crawl and wriggle and foam with rage,
Through dusk tradition and ballad age.

John Greenleaf Whittier, "The Double-Headed Snake of Newbury"

Dragons! Fire-belching damsel devourers mortally skewered upon a valiant knight's lance, or ethereal serpentine deities wafting languorously through the skies in celestial tranquillity. Vermiform monsters with coils of steel, or winged wonders with jewel-encrusted scales. Bat-winged nightmares that terrorize and desecrate with volcanic gullets of flame, or polychromatic dream beasts soaring heavenward upon iridescent plumes of crystalline glory. Personifications of malevolence or beneficence, paganism or purity, death and devastation, life and fertility, good or evil. All of these varied, contradictory concepts are embodied and embedded within that single magical word.

Although there have been many books devoted to dragons, they have focused largely upon the symbolic, sociological, or geographical significance of dragons. In contrast, this volume takes as its theme the great variety and classification of dragon types—delineating their evolutionary transformation from simple, serpentine forms to much more complex, specialized beasts.

For although the winged, four-legged, flame-spewing horror of classical mythology may well be the most famous type of dragon in the Western world, it is far from being the only type on record—a fundamental facet of dragon lore, yet seldom noted (let alone emphasized) in any previous works. Worms and lindorms, wyverns, winged serpents and sky-borne dragon-gods, the guivre and the six-legged tarasque, water-spouting gargouilles, many-headed hydras, and toad-incubated cockatrices—and numberless others—also belong to the dynasty of the dragon.

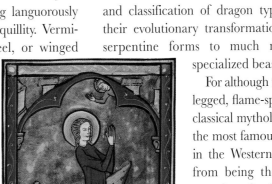

St. Margaret, who was swallowed by Satan disguised as a dragon, emerges unharmed from his stomach.

Paolo Uccello's version of the St. George story (c.1460) shows the dragon with two legs, rather than the usual four, but its wings bear the eyespots lacking in other versions.

A second impetus when preparing this book was to present a vivid retelling of some of the most spectacular, and also some of the less familiar, dragon legends—all too often relegated to a meager, lifeless summary. Revitalizing the dynamic confrontations of these creatures with mankind vigorously transforms mythology's most formidable fauna from intangible monsters of the imagination into rampaging reptilians as alive and authentic as anything that strides, slithers, swims, or soars through the grim world of reality.

This objective has been supplemented by the incorporation of an array of paintings, jewelry, archaeological artifacts, architectural curiosities, and engravings. Many artistic renditions of the dragons in famous myths and legends bear little resemblance to the traditional written descriptions; but who could find fault with an opponent of St. George that looks unexpectedly like a wyvern when it is depicted with such breathtaking splendor by a painter of Uccello's caliber, or even

with an incongruously walruslike Cetus when executed in the glorious style of Piero di Cosimo?

Last, the compelling possibility is explored that, whereas some dragons were clearly inspired by real-life animals long familiar to the zoological world, others may be based upon mysterious living creatures still awaiting formal discovery by science. Are these the elusive, corporeal dragons of tomorrow?

Setting out to reveal not only the dragons of the past and the present, but also those of the future, this book assimilates eye-opening information and thought-provoking concepts that should stir the imagination of devoted dragonophiles everywhere. Or, as the compiler of bestiaries Edward Topsell wrote in 1608 in his *Historie of Serpents*: "Among all the kindes of Serpents, there is none comparable to the Dragon, or that affordeth and yeeldeth so much plentifull matter in history for the ample discovery of the nature thereof: and therefore heerein I must borrow more time…than peradventure the Reader would be willing to spare…[but] I will strive to make the description pleasant, with variable history…"

SERPENT DRAGONS

Many dracontologists consider that the belief in dragons was inspired by sightings of large serpents: that dragons "evolved" from snakes. If so, then the first stage in this evolution is represented by the serpent dragons. Usually associated with rivers, lakes, or the open seas, these are huge, limbless and wingless snakelike entities, readily recognized by their dragonesque heads, which often sport horns, and their long crocodilian jaws.

THE CURSE OF THE LAMBTON WORM

*On the morning of Easter Sunday, 1420,
everyone from the village of Washington, close to
the River Wear in County Durham, England,
was hurrying to church—everyone, that is, except
John Lambton, the young, dissolute heir to
nearby Lambton Castle.*

Eschewing spiritual solace and observation of the sabbath for more material, disrespectful pleasures, he was fishing in the river, ignoring the disapproving glances of the churchgoers. As the morning turned into afternoon with not a single fish taking his bait, however, Lambton's mood darkened, and he cursed aloud with blasphemous abandon at his ill fortune.

As if bidden by this profane outburst, a ripple shivered across the river's surface. Moments later, the young man felt something tug sharply at his line, but it was not a fish. When he hauled it up out of the water, he thought at first that it was some form of aquatic worm or leech, small yet elongated, with slimy black skin. Then it raised its head and looked at him, and even the brash Lambton caught his breath in horror, for his unexpected catch had the head of a dragon—and the face of a devil.

Its jaws were slender, brimming with long needlelike teeth, and evil-smelling fluid oozed from nine gill-like slits on either side of its neck; but all that Lambton saw were its eyes. Like icy coals they glittered, snaring his own in a glacial, mesmeric trance, and as he gazed helplessly into them, all the sins of his wasted youth danced in their malevolent darkness, like mocking wraiths.

John Lambton had initially planned to keep whatever he caught, but all he wanted to do now was rid himself of this loathsome creature, and he lost no time in casting it down a nearby well. From that moment on, he was a changed person, seeking redemption and salvation for his former misdeeds, a mission that led him a few years later to go on a pilgrimage to the Holy Land. And so he left the village and his castle far behind, but he also left behind a monstrous manifestation of his former wickedness.

Unknown to Lambton, his captive had thrived within the well's gloomy confines, growing steadily and stealthily larger and ever more powerful. One morning, some of the villagers

The legend of the Lambton worm and its intrepid slayer has lived on, and the story still appears in many books of folk tales.

from Washington spied a strange trail, glistening with acidic slime, that led from the well to a hill close by. Intrigued, they followed the trail, and a terrible sight met their eyes.

So huge that the coils of its snakelike body enfolded the hill nine times, a hideous limbless dragon of the type known as a worm or orm lay basking in the sunshine. Livid slime seared the grass under its body, and poisonous vapor spiraling out of its mouth withered the leaves on the surrounding trees.

Thus began the Lambton worm's grisly reign of terror, during which it laid waste Washington's once verdant countryside, devoured livestock and even small children, and turned the villagers into captives within their homes, frightened to set foot outside their doors lest they encounter their land's deadly despoiler. In desperation, with an ancient gesture customary when plagued by a marauding dragon, they attempted to pacify the monster with an offering of milk.

A huge trough was filled with fresh milk and placed in the courtyard of Lambton Castle, where it could be readily seen by the worm. As expected, the creature rapidly slithered forth and lapped up the offering. For the rest of that day and all through the night, it remained passively wrapped around its chosen hillside retreat; but when no milk was forthcoming on the following morning, it rampaged in fury, while the terrified villagers cowered in their

The Lambton worm is daily recalled in Washington, for there is a pub of that name, whose colorful sign acts as a constant reminder of the story.

houses. So from that time onward, every cow in the village was milked exclusively to provide a daily tribute sufficient to satisfy the worm.

Every so often, a few villagers braver than the rest attempted to dispatch their serpentine enslaver with sword or lance. But even if they succeeded in slicing the beast in half, the halves immediately joined together again, yielding an intact, highly irascible worm that rarely gave its attackers the opportunity either to repeat their ploy or to flee the fray.

Years passed by until at last John Lambton returned home. He was horrified to discover the worm's baneful presence and determined to rid

his land of the evil that had been inflicted upon it by his own youthful decadence; so he sought the advice of a wise old witch. She informed him that he would only succeed in killing the monster if he wore a special suit of armor, with sharp blades all over the surface, and if he confronted it in the middle of the river where he had originally caught it.

There was, however, a price to pay for success. After slaying the worm, he must also kill the next living thing he met. If he failed to do this, the Lambton lineage would be cursed, and for nine generations no heir to the Lambton estates would die in his bed.

Heeding all that the witch had told him, John Lambton at once arranged for a suit of spike-adorned armor to be prepared for him and set forth in it to engage in battle with his dreadful foe. By swift and subtle swordplay, he enticed the worm into the fast-flowing water of the River Wear. Once there, the worm seized him in its coils; but the more it sought to crush him, the more severely the razor-sharp blades on Lambton's

During the 1930s, cigarette cards were issued portraying English legends, including that of the Lambton worm; today these cards are valuable, not only for themselves, but also as a record of folklore.

suit sliced into its body. Aided by his sword thrusts, the blades eventually sliced the worm into several segments and, before they could recombine, the river's swift current bore them away. Thus was the fearsome Lambton worm destroyed.

Rejoicing, the young man returned home to Lambton Castle, but although he had vanquished the worm, its curse lingered. His old father, ecstatically happy to see that his son had survived his formidable encounter, was the first living thing to run to greet him. When he saw this, John Lambton became pale with fear, knowing that if he was to secure the safety of his descendants he must kill his own father—but he simply could not do so. Instead, he killed his most faithful dog, in the hope that this sacrifice would be enough, but it was not, and for the next nine generations, every heir to Lambton Castle met a tragic end.

Although the worm had gone, forever after the legend of this terrible serpent dragon would be associated with the name of Lambton.

The Guivre and the Gargouille

Dragons are not noted for shy, bashful behavior, which is why the guivre is so unusual an example.

In medieval times, France was regularly blighted by these enormous serpent dragons, which inhabited woodlands, forests, rivers, streams, and even deep wells.

Many serpent dragons were infamous for their venomous breath, which would poison anything that inhaled its putrid fumes and would shrivel the grass upon which these loathsome reptiles wriggled. The guivre's breath, however, was exceptionally toxic, spontaneously generating virulent plagues and diseases. Wherever there was a guivre, there was death and destruction, and France feared for its very survival. Until, that is, an extraordinary discovery was made that offered a highly novel means of combating these terrible monsters.

One warm afternoon, a young farmer, hot and tired from a hard day spent laboring in the fields, stripped off his clothes and plunged into the cool, inviting waters of the local river for a refreshing swim. Half an hour later, feeling greatly invigorated, he stepped out of the water on to the riverbank and was about to dry himself when the bushes were pushed aside and out slithered a huge guivre.

As he stared in horror at this monstrosity, so great was the farmer's fear that he was unable to move and expected at any moment to be

The serpent dragons in this early engraving show the likely appearance of the water-spouting gargouille, whose existence was inspired by periods of severe flooding, and the guivre, the embodiment of virulent epidemics.

asphyxiated or devoured, or both. The guivre raised its hideous horned head and glared down at him, ready to open its terrible jaws and confirm his worst expectations, but when it saw his brawny, muscular body and realized that he was naked, an astonishing change took place. Instead of attacking, the monster seemed to recoil, its face suffused with color as it frantically sought to direct its eyes away from the lusty, unclothed figure. Incredibly, the guivre was blushing. In a matter of seconds, the mighty serpent dragon had fled, gliding rapidly away through the bushes. The amazed farmer remained motionless for several minutes, unsure as to whether it would return and perplexed as to why it had fled.

It was not long before others discovered that although guivres would not hesitate to kill fully clothed men, the sight of a naked man scared them witless. This remarkable piece of knowledge was utilized to good effect, ensuring that no guivre could ever again come close enough to human habitation to spread disease and death.

Medieval buildings are rich in gargoyles—spouts designed to drain water from parapet gutters—such as this one on the cathedral of Notre-Dame in Paris.

Indeed, guivres eventually disappeared from France. Some say that they simply died out; others that they migrated to lands where the climate was not so conducive to open-air bathing.

Not all dragons spew flame or noxious vapor; some spout fountains of water to equally devastating effect. In the year 520, Rouen, the capital of Normandy, was under siege, not by a foreign army, not even by some pestilence, but by something far more menacing. It had emerged one pale morning from the waters of the Seine.

At first a great scaled head appeared, borne upon a long neck like that of some strange reptilian swan. It was equipped with a slender snout and jaws and had heavy brows encircling a pair of eyes that gleamed like moonstones. And as the waters cascaded from its shoulders, the creature revealed itself as an aquatic serpent dragon of colossal size. It was sheathed in a fine mail of pale, glaucous scalloping and sported a pair of membranous fins in place of true limbs.

After surveying its surroundings for a few moments, the monster opened its mouth, and from its throat sprang a tremendous jet of water that engulfed the countryside all around in an immense tidal wave. From that day, this terrifying creature—swiftly dubbed the *gargouille*, or "gargler," by the local people—mercilessly saturated the land with great fountains of water until the entire region was imperiled by severe flooding. Farmlands were devastated, and countless people perished. Many were devoured by the dragon, and others met their death by drowning when it wantonly capsized their boats as they sailed upon the Seine.

St. Romain, archbishop of Rouen, watched this unfolding catastrophe with mounting horror and knew that he must act if the land were to be saved from the gargouille's dominion of destruction. Learning that the creature lived in a cave in the banks of the Seine, he decided to confront it there and to do whatever was necessary to quell its tyranny forever. Yet despite pleading for

Gargoyles are usually grotesque birds or beasts similar to this dragonlike figure on Notre-Dame. They tend to sit on their haunches on the parapet, projecting out several feet so that the water is spouted well clear of the base of the building.

assistance from the region's besieged inhabitants, he could not find anyone to accompany him on his noble quest until he encountered a prisoner condemned to death for murder. Since his life was already forfeit, the prisoner had nothing to lose by facing a deadly water dragon in its grim lair, so he willingly agreed to help the archbishop.

No sooner had the two brave men reached its cave than the dreadful gargouille appeared, rearing above them with jaws agape as it prepared to disgorge from its gullet a teeming cataract that would blast them away to a cold, watery grave. But even as the lethal tide bubbled upward in the monster's throat, St. Romain stepped forward, raised his arms high above his head, and placed two fingers against one another in the form of the Cross. Instantly, the terrible beast sank down, its threatened torrent seeping harmlessly from between its jaws in an insipid trickle, its foaming fury thoroughly extinguished.

So complete was the transformation that the dragon even allowed St. Romain to bind its neck with his stole, enabling the murderer to lead it passively back into Rouen. Following the gargouille's arrival, the vengeful townsfolk gathered around it in droves, intent upon annihilating their one-time persecutor. And, in accordance with their demands, the monster was put to death, not by water but by fire, until only a great heap of ashes remained to testify to its existence.

These were cast into the River Seine, but even today there are ample reminders of the fearsome gargouille. Deriving both their name and their water-spouting talents from this infamous monster are the gargoyles, whose grotesque figures adorn countless churches and other buildings in France and in countries all around the world.

As for the murderer, in recognition of his bravery and his loyalty to the archbishop, he was pardoned and set free; and for many years thereafter, every archbishop of Rouen was permitted by law to pardon one criminal each year on Ascension Day.

Jormungander, the Midgard Serpent

The Aesir—Norse mythology's splendid array of gallant warrior gods—confronted numerous monsters, but none to compare with Jormungander, the gigantic Midgard Serpent.

Spawned by Loki, god of evil, its coils stretched across the earth as far as the eye could see, and its hideous dragon's head and limitless neck towered over the land and mountains like a scaly ebony pillar surmounted by the visage of death itself. Little wonder, then, that when this frightful apparition was brought before the Aesir, Odin the All-Wise cast it far out into the deepest ocean, where its thrashing bulk was soon enveloped by the turbulence of the waves.

Yet although it had disappeared from sight, Jormungander did not vanish from existence. On the contrary. Deep within its watery domain, far beyond the realms of gods and men, it grew even larger until eventually its mighty coils encircled the globe, its jaws grasping its tail like a colossal ouroboros. Here it was destined to remain until Ragnarok, the Day of the Last Battle. Only then

An ouroboros depicted in a 15th-century French manuscript.

would Jormungander be freed, and on that day it would confront the mightiest of the Aesir—Thor, god of thunder.

Long before this cataclysmic encounter, however, these two formidable combatants were destined to cross paths on two separate occasions. The first meeting took place during a visit by Thor to Utgardhaloki, the king of the giants who were long-standing enemies of the Aesir. Seeing an opportunity to belittle the mighty Thor, Utgardhaloki challenged him to a trio of physical trials. These feats were, in fact, impossible for anyone to accomplish—god or giant—but the king was skilled in the magic and art of illusion and had cloaked their true nature, making them appear commonplace in order to deceive his visitor. One of the trials seemed particularly demeaning. Mocking Thor's renowned strength, Utgardhaloki expressed doubt that the god could even pick up his pet cat. Greatly angered, Thor grasped the animal on both sides and, retaining the spitting ball of fury in a firm grip of his powerful hands, attempted to lift it off the ground; but the

Thor battling with the Midgard Serpent *was painted by Henry Fuseli in 1788.*

cat did not move. Heave and haul as he might, Thor could not raise the animal as much as an inch into the air. Utgardhaloki laughed loudly at this incongruous sight, enraging Thor and spurring him on to make one last attempt. With every sinew taut and every muscle straining with the exertion, Thor pulled at the king's unyielding pet until his fingers felt as if they were about to snap, but he succeeded in lifting only one of its paws a fraction off the floor.

Thor was equally embarrassed by the other tests. Famed for his great drinking prowess, he failed in three drafts to quaff a horn of mead that Utgardhaloki's subjects reputedly emptied in two or less. And offering the ultimate indignity, he was brought to his knees in a wrestling match with the king's childhood nurse, a feeble old woman.

Ashamed and humiliated, Thor left the kingdom of Utgardhaloki the following morning and was escorted far beyond its borders by the king himself. Only then, with his land safely distant from any anger that Thor might seek to vent upon it, did Utgardhaloki confess the truth concerning the trials with which he had taunted the god.

The horn had been connected to the oceans, and although, therefore, Thor could never have succeeded in entirely quaffing its contents, his measure of achievement had been so profound that he had created the world's first ebb tide. As for the "feeble old nurse," she was none other than Old Age, and no one, however strong, can ever conquer her.

Most astonishing of all, however, was the strength Thor had demonstrated with Utgardhaloki's cat, for this was not a cat at all. Its feline form was just an illusion, deftly woven by the king to conceal the true identity of an entirely different creature—the serpent that encircled the world,

Jormungander. When Thor had succeeded in lifting one of the cat's "paws" off the ground, he had actually lifted the head and tail of the great Midgard Serpent, a feat so astounding that Utgardhaloki had scarcely been able to hide his horror with his false laughter.

Learning how he had been tricked, Thor would certainly have slain the giant king with his magical hammer, Miolnir, but as soon as he had spoken his final words, Utgardhaloki vanished: his presence accompanying Thor's departure had itself been only an illusion.

A Viking silver bracelet, in the form of a double-headed dragon, or amphisbaena, dating from the 11th century.

Many years later, Thor and another giant, Hymir, grandfather of Tyr, god of war, were fishing on the ocean in Hymir's boat, and Thor was using an entire ox head as bait. Suddenly, something immensely powerful seized the head and began hauling it down through the waves, with the hook firmly embedded in its jaw. Thor was well aware that there was only one creature able to exert such force—the Midgard Serpent.

Remembering how this monster had made him appear weak and foolish at the court of Utgardhaloki, he relished the opportunity to haul the serpent dragon out of the ocean and hurl it on the shore. Pulling upon the line with every atom of his strength, Thor battled with the giant creature for what seemed like an age to the petrified Hymir, but eventually Jormungander tired, and Thor seemed set to achieve his long-standing ambition.

The creature's immense, repulsive head rose up through the water, and Thor whirled his hammer Miolnir to strike the fatal blow; but at that moment, Hymir's nerve snapped. The sight of the dreadful visage so close to his own face was too much for him, and without hesitation he cut Thor's line. Instantly, the Midgard Serpent sank down through the waves, while Thor could only rage impotently at having been thwarted again.

Countless ages passed in the realm of mortals, but to the Aesir it seemed only the blink of an eye since the world had begun when Ragnarok arrived. This was the long-awaited Day of the Last Battle, with god against giant, deity against demon, man against monster, and Thor, god of thunder, against Jormungander.

Jormungander about to swallow the ox's head as illustrated in an Icelandic manuscript dating from 1680.

The ocean writhed as the colossal dragon uncoiled itself to come ashore to do battle with the only being capable of offering it a worthy challenge. Thor was waiting, and their final combat began. The earth shook with the violence of the dragon's unceasing assault upon his adversary, and the heavens were set alight as Thor hurled scorching thunderbolts and bright javelins of lightning at his deadly foe.

With a final war cry, Thor raised Miolnir high above his head, whirling it round and round until the skies wheeled in a giddy vortex—then he plunged it down upon the bony head of the dragon with a crashing blow that echoed right around the world. Fatally wounded, the Midgard Serpent emitted an earsplitting blast of rage and pain before sinking lifeless to the ground.

Thor had conquered the most terrible enemy ever to challenge the Aesir, but so, too, had Jormungander conquered the mightiest of their number. For only moments after slaying the serpent dragon, Thor fell dead alongside it, asphyxiated by the fetid cloud of venom exhaled with the great beast's final breath. For two enemies so evenly matched, the outcome seemed as fitting as it was inevitable.

KITCHI-AT'HUSIS AND THE GIANT LEECH

The mythology of the many tribes of native American Indians contains numerous aquatic serpent dragons, with names as diverse as the water panther, water bison, giant leech, water grizzly, great water snake, and horned serpent.

Wise shamans could occasionally transform themselves into these frightening entities, and one particularly dramatic confrontation between two such magicians took place long ago in the waters of Boyden Lake in Washington County, Maine.

Challenged by a rival shaman, the Passamaquoddy's highly skilled wizard, Medshelemet, met him beneath the lake's surface to do battle in a traditional magical duel, and each instantly transformed himself into a selected shape.

Medshelemet took on the terrifying guise of a huge sluglike creature known as the *weewilmekq*, or giant leech. Its slimy body was patterned in a vivid checked design, and its flattened head bore a pair of sharp curving horns and a sucker with a serrated edge, with which it would pump out the tissue and fluids of its living victim until all that remained was an empty, dried-out husk. In response, his wily opponent changed into an even more horrific beast, the great 40-foot (12-m) long water serpent called

In the form of the giant leech weewilmekq, *the shaman Medshelemet fought and defeated his rival shaman disguised as a horned serpent.*

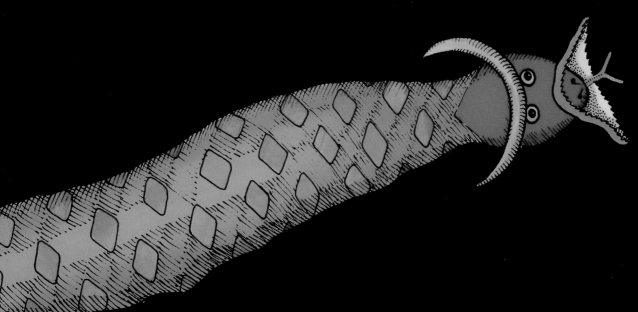

Kitchi-at'husis, with shimmering scaly coils, a pair of deerlike antlers sprouting from its skull, and such venomous fangs that their merest touch brought instant death.

The two monsters were well matched, and at first they warily circled around each other, neither of them willing to initiate the attack. Then suddenly, before the eye could register any movement, they had thrown themselves upon one another, thrashing like dismembered tentacles as the water swirled around in a maelstrom of fury. The *weewilmekq* aimed for the neck of Kitchi-at'husis—once attached there, it would be safe from the snake's fangs, and its own deadly sucker would have time to perform its vampirelike function. Kitchi-at'husis recoiled as its attacker struck, but the *weewilmekq* was swifter, anchoring itself securely to the massive serpent's nape. Its sucker immediately began to rasp away great slivers of flesh as the maddened Kitchi-at'husis twisted about wildly in a vain bid to shake off its parasitic opponent and to deliver a strike with at least a single venomous fang.

But as its blood ebbed away, the great serpent weakened. Suddenly, a convulsive shudder jolted through its coils, a spasm of lacerating pain, and then Kitchi-at'husis was dead, its body drifting limply down to the lake bottom. The *weewilmekq*, transformed back into Medshelemet, triumphantly raised on high his vanquished rival's body, which retained its snake guise even in death. The sucker had proved mightier than the fang.

Another voracious leech dragon as large as a house, with white stripes crisscrossing its crimson body, frequented the conflux of the Valley River with the Hiwassee, at Murphy, North Carolina. Its aquatic hideaway was known to the local Cherokees as *Tlanusi'yi*, "the place of the leech," and such was the violence of the monster's wavelike undulations when swimming that the water would be churned into a boiling ferment of foam.

Anyone who came too close to this creature was unlikely to survive the encounter. In seconds, the leech dragon would vomit a spray of foul liquid over its luckless victim, who was then hauled down into the riverbed's evil-smelling ooze. What happened there remained a mystery, which is probably just as well. For in due course, the victim's corpse would be found lying on the riverbank—with its nose and ears torn off.

REGULUS AND THE
CARTHAGINIAN SERPENT GIANT

*Not only is it likely that many legends of serpent
dragons were inspired by encounters with real
snakes, but it is also possible that some such snakes
were far greater in size than any known today.*

The history of Regulus and the Carthaginian
serpent giant seems to bear this out. A little more
than 250 years before the birth of Christ, at the
time of the first Punic War (264–241 B.C.), Rome
was engaged in a particularly bitter conflict with
the ancient city of Carthage over the control of the
island of Sicily.

The Roman army, under one of its most
renowned and fearless generals, Marcus Atilius
Regulus, had progressed triumphantly toward
Carthage, which lay near present-day Tunis in
North Africa. They had reached the River
Bagrada when, without warning, the army was
confronted by a native foe that was far more
deadly than anything Carthage could have
summoned to its aid.

As Regulus's battalions, bristling with hand
weapons and war machines, attempted to cross
the Bagrada, an enormous snake suddenly reared
up from the reed beds fringing its muddy banks.
Higher and higher, its huge flattened head rose,
and the men fell back in great alarm and not a
little fear at the sight of such a monstrous form.

The immense serpent's eyes glowed like
lanterns, and the soldiers' ears were filled with the
sound of its sibilant fury as its bifurcated tongue
flickered back and forth along its half-open jaws
which brimmed with fangs. Never before had the
soldiers seen such a beast. As they cautiously
watched from a distance, the enormous snake
emerged farther from the cover of the reeds.

Coil after coil of powerful, scale-
spangled muscle rose up from the
river's murky waters as the vast
creature, which they estimated
to be at least 100 feet (30 m) in
length, gazed at the force
assembled upon the bank. Yet it
made no effort to approach—so
what were they to do?

After a swift consultation
with his officers, Regulus
decided to cross the river
some distance farther along,
away from its overseer; so
the men marched upstream

*An early representation of a
"boa" shows it with a hugely
distended belly consuming a
child; significantly, it also has the
typical arrow-shaped tail of a dragon.*

toward a suitable spot. Looking back, they realized that the snake had vanished, and without further ado started to cross. But no sooner had the first man entered the river than the water around him began to boil. Seconds later, the evil head of the monstrous snake appeared, seized the hapless soldier in its viselike jaws, enveloped him in the merciless folds of its coils, and dragged him down to his death beneath the water. The same thing happened to the second man who tried to cross, and to the third, and the fourth. Each of them was abducted by the serpent and drowned.

During the struggle that followed to dispatch their nemesis in straightforward hand combat, dozens of other men also lost their lives, until the threat posed by this inhuman adversary spurred Regulus to adopt a drastic, and dramatic, strategy.

Although the serpent was a single entity, in battle terms it was so unassailable that it could be considered to constitute a fortress, so Regulus decided to confront it in precisely the same way that his army would besiege a real fortress.

The siege ballistae—massive catapults capable of hurling heavy rocks—were wheeled forward and their missiles released, bombarding the giant

In 1934, there were reports of farmers near Syracuse, in Sicily, being menaced by a huge and unusual snake that looked much like a dinosaur; hunting parties were organized, and it was later killed.

snake with an avalanche of boulders. The ballistae were reloaded and fired again and again, as their serpentine target writhed in pain and shock at the torrent of blows leveled at it. It began to retreat, its body sinking beneath the surface of the river, but suddenly a particularly large, sharp-edged rock hurtled downward and crashed with full force directly between the beast's eyes, shattering its skull and killing it outright.

As the serpent's body collapsed, the eerie glow in its eyes dimmed and its spade-shaped head dropped onto the bank, almost at the feet of the soldiers. A large part of its inert body lay out of the water as well; so when Regulus was convinced that their terrible opponent had truly expired, he commanded his men to drag it clear of the river and skin it. The snake was found to measure an astonishing 120 feet (37 m)—four times as long as any snake known anywhere in the world in modern times.

So magnificent a trophy could hardly be discarded; so upon Regulus's victorious return to Rome, with great ceremony he presented the skin and jaws of the Carthaginian serpent giant to the city. In recognition of his valiant endeavor and

Tales are told in India of attacks by gigantic pythons; this 19th-century magazine illustration depicts a recorded attack by a specimen more than 62 feet (18 m) long.

African rock pythons can grow to a length of more than 23 feet (7 m) and, with their hinged jaws, are able to devour large prey, such as this gazelle.

acclaimed success in slaying such a monster, an ovation was granted to the general, an extraordinary honor that was recorded by Roman historians. As for the serpent, its remains were placed on display in one of the temples on Capitol Hill, where they could be seen until the time of the Numantine War against the Iberian Celts in 133 B.C., when they disappeared.

The identity of the serpent has never been ascertained. It could have been an African rock python, but even allowing for the marked climatic changes that have taken place there in the past 2,000 years, none is thought to have existed in this part of the continent. Furthermore, in parts of Africa where rock pythons are now found, no specimen even remotely as long as Regulus's antagonist has ever been conclusively recorded.

PERSEUS AND THE DRAGON OF POSEIDON

Perseus, the valiant warrior son of the god Zeus and the Greek princess Danaë, was returning from the far end of the earth to his home on the island of Seriphos.

His bold quest had been successful, and inside a sturdy, well-sealed sack, he was carrying a matchless wedding gift for his king, Polydectes—the head of the gorgon Medusa. This hideous monster, whose hair comprised a seething mass of living serpents, had eyes endowed with the terrible power to turn to stone anyone who gazed into them. Armed with this petrifying trophy, Polydectes would be invincible, and thus, Perseus hoped, would look kindly upon him.

As Perseus flew over Ethiopia, borne through the sky by the winged sandals lent to him by the messenger of the gods, Hermes, he looked down and saw a young maiden chained to a cliff overlooking the wild ocean. She was unquestionably of royal blood, with golden hair and a flowing white gown that the raging waves tore at with fingers of foam.

Swooping down until he was hovering directly in front of the fair prisoner, Perseus saw that her eyes, filled with terror, were fixed upon the ocean. Here, it was evident, the instrument of her destruction would appear—but what could it be, and why was she fettered here?

Piero di Cosimo's painting (c.1515) shows Perseus both in the air and slaying the dragon. He wears Hermes' winged sandals and Hades' helmet, which made him invisible. He carried Medusa's head in a sack. To avoid being turned to stone when he slew her, he guided himself by her reflection in a mirror. Eventually, he gave the head to Athena, who placed it on her shield.

Perseus's appearance was so unexpected that, despite her fearful fascination with the sea below, the tethered maiden found herself gazing instead at the handsome prince suspended in mid-air before her. And so she revealed to him the grim events that had led to her doom.

She was the princess Andromeda, daughter of Cassiopeia, the vain, impetuous wife of Ethiopia's king Cepheus. Not long before, in a fit of pride, Cassiopeia had proclaimed that she was even more beautiful than those incomparably lovely sea nymphs known as the Nereids. Incensed by this unprecedented affront, the mighty sea god Poseidon had called forth from the ocean's abyss Cetus, a monstrous fork-tailed serpent dragon, and commanded it to wreak havoc upon the kingdom of Cepheus and the hapless Cassiopeia.

Countless people and livestock had already been devoured by this rampaging manifestation of divine retribution and, according to an oracle consulted by the panicking monarchs, the slaughter would continue until their entire land was obliterated unless their daughter Andromeda was sacrificed to Cetus. Only then would Poseidon's wrath be assuaged.

And so, with breaking hearts, the tragic king and queen were forced to do the unthinkable. Andromeda was taken to the highest cliff overlooking the realm of Poseidon, and there she was

A beautiful Nereid, or sea nymph, one of Poseidon's entourage, rides on the back of a sea horse on the chased lid of a small box dating from c.130 B.C.

shackled to await her terrible death. Scarcely had the despairing Andromeda ended her sad tale before vivid confirmation of its veracity began to materialize. Something was rising up through the waves from the bed of the dark ocean. At first, it appeared as an enormous crimson shadow, rippling and shuddering as it grew larger. Then it seemed like a bright scarlet whirlpool of blood, twisting and spinning as it neared the surface. Suddenly it burst through the water, and the greatest horror ever to emerge from the domain of the sea god was at last visible in all its terrible magnificence.

Cetus resembled a bizarre serpent whale of colossal size, whose gigantic coils of ocher and aquamarine were marked by countless rings of impenetrable scales. Its head, however, was more like that of a hound, and two immense ivory tusks similar to those of a walrus projected from its jaws. Although it was limbless, a pair of ornate membranous fins fluttered about its broad, plated chest; but most spectacular of all was the brilliant, blood-red crest set upon the crown of its skull like a fiery pennant, whose swirling motion when submerged beneath the water had yielded the illusion of a crimson shadow and a scarlet vortex during its ascent.

The sea dragon's eyes glittered with malevolent exultation. Amid their internal flames of cold turquoise fire, the puppetlike reflection of the princess soundlessly shrieked and struggled to escape from its mirrored bonds. The reflection grew steadily larger as Andromeda's nemesis swam toward her, its head and neck held high above the waves like the prow of a galleon.

As for Perseus, Cetus dismissed him from its attention as a tiger would discount an insect buzzing overhead—and in so doing sealed its fate. Just as even the tiniest gnat has a potent sting, so too was Perseus equipped with a sturdy sword, the one that had only recently parted the head of Medusa from her armor-encased neck and winged shoulders.

Intent upon its merciless progression toward the seemingly defenseless princess, the dragon failed to spy her airborne protector soaring beneath its wide-open jaws. Then Perseus's blade stabbed through an unprotected juncture of the plates covering its chest and plunged deep into its heart.

Once, twice, three times, the warrior's sword pierced its pulsating depths, and Cetus collapsed in upon itself, its vital essence ebbing away in rivulets of darkening, congealing blood. Soon it was all over, and the lifeless carcass sank beneath the surface of the ocean. Exhausted, but greatly exhilarated, Perseus swiftly freed Andromeda

The serpent dragon of the Perseus myth may have been inspired by rare sightings of the oarfish, a deep-sea creature that can reach 60 feet (18 m) in length. Its fins are coral-red, and the dorsal fin can be raised on the head to form a crest.

from her bindings. Tearfully she embraced him, and when he looked into her eyes their unspoken words assured him that his quest for the wife of his dreams had ended before it had even begun.

But what happened to the head of Medusa? Following a resplendent wedding in Cepheus's revitalized kingdom, Perseus and his bride returned in triumph to Seriphos, where he had intended to present his trophy of the gorgon's head to King Polydectes to mark his forthcoming marriage.

But to his great dismay and anger, Perseus discovered that, in his absence, Polydectes had been inflicting his unwelcome attentions upon Perseus's own mother, Danaë. Indeed, it transpired that the king's supposed plans for marriage to another had been nothing but a sham, a devious ploy to send Perseus on a quest that seemed destined to end in his death, so enabling Polydectes to pursue Danaë—the true object of his desire—without fear. There was only one way to bring this travesty to a close.

Perseus demanded an audience with Polydectes and, taking Medusa's head out of the sack, showed him his wedding gift. Then Perseus strode out of the palace, leaving the courtiers to remove the stone statue that had once been their king.

LEVIATHAN

"That crooked serpent…the dragon that is in the sea." Thus was Leviathan, the most stupendous and spectacular of God's beasts, described in the Book of Isaiah.

On the fifth day of Creation, the day upon which God shaped and breathed life into all of the creatures of the sea, He fashioned the mighty and magnificent serpent dragon Leviathan to serve as the ruler of this vast marine kingdom. The boundless coils of its immensely long body were encased in an impervious sheathing of overlapping scales, and it thrashed through the water with such explosive force that the ocean depths boiled like a fathomless cauldron. Its incandescent eyes, more than 300 in number, illuminated the seas beyond and the skies above with their radiant glow. Seething steam jetted forth from its flared nostrils, and brilliant tongues of fire flickered from its enormous jaws.

No mortal weapon could penetrate the shimmering armor of Leviathan's scales, no living thing on earth could oppose its might, and nothing could ignite a flicker of fear within its firm, indestructible heart. Dragons a thousand miles in length were devoured like mice, and the waters of the River Jordan emptied themselves into its cavernous maw, which brimmed with teeth of terrifying proportion and quantity. In the wake of its passage through the ocean, the waves glittered as if spangled with phosphorescent hoar frost, and all the world marveled at the wonder of Leviathan.

Initially, God created a pair of these fantastic beasts, but when it became clear that their collective power was so awesome that the entire world was threatened by the prospect of a race of such creatures ultimately establishing itself, God destroyed one of them. As a further measure, He created the stickleback. This tiny, seemingly innocuous fish was specifically designed by God to counter the wilder excesses of the surviving Leviathan, to whom, as compensation for the loss of its partner, He granted immortality.

Since then, during the final three hours of every day, God has played with Leviathan, disporting with His gargantuan creation—and this will continue until the Day of Judgment. Only then will Leviathan die, slain by the Archangel Gabriel, after which its flesh will serve as food for the righteous, who will be housed within a glorious tent fabricated from a portion of its iridescent scaly hide. The remainder will be spread over the walls of Jerusalem, from which its radiance will pour forth to illuminate every corner of the globe.

Leviathan's immense size and power is forcefully conveyed in illustrator Arthur Rackham's fine watercolor of the great serpent dragon in his book of fairy stories.

Over the centuries, biblical scholars have devoted great time and energy to the riddle of Leviathan's identity. Could this majestic symbol of God's power have been based upon a real creature? The most popular candidate is the Nile crocodile, which did exist in the Middle East during biblical times. Whereas Leviathan was marine, however, this species is restricted to fresh water. And although it certainly possesses a scaly, elongated body of considerable (but hardly colossal) size, a powerful neck, glittering eyes, and numerous large and sharp teeth, the Nile crocodile lacks the smoking nostrils and the fins of Leviathan.

Whales constitute another possible identity for Leviathan. Yet whereas several species are indeed huge, relatively streamlined in shape, and equipped with fins and sometimes large teeth, as well as blowholes that spout spray upward when they exhale air (which may explain Leviathan's smoking nostrils), they are neither scaly nor shiny-eyed, and their necks are short.

More recently, a particularly thought-provoking contender has reared its head. Could Leviathan have been based upon some mysterious, still undiscovered sea beast currently responsible for various sea serpent reports?

Leviathan's biblical description, and many illustrations based upon it, certainly do recall various elongated, reptilian mystery creatures that have been spied by reliable eye-witnesses in many marine localities. It is particularly reminiscent of a supposedly long-extinct form of dragonlike marine reptile, known as the mosasaur (*see p.115*). Could an undiscovered modern-day species of mosasaur be the explanation for the saltwater serpent dragon found in the Bible?

Perhaps there will yet come a day when science obtains a complete specimen of one of the ocean's elusive reptilian sea monsters for formal study and classification. Then, at last, we may know the identity of Leviathan itself, the greatest sea monster of all.

Another zoological enigma from the Bible, closely linked with Leviathan, is Behemoth. Although Leviathan is traditionally considered to be unique and male, according to the Book of

The imagination of the French printmaker and artist Gustave Doré was fired by the story of Leviathan; this woodcut appeared in his edition of the Bible published in 1860.

William Blake's hand-colored engraving of Leviathan and Behemoth is among his illustrations for the Book of Job (1825), which mark the peak of his work as an artist.

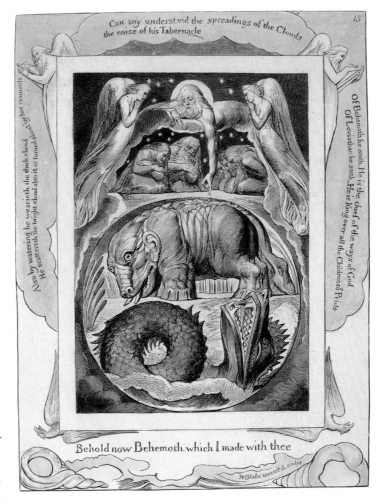

Behold now Behemoth which I made with thee

WBlake invent & sculpt

Enoch in the Apocrypha, it is female, and its male counterpart is Behemoth, which inhabits an immeasurable desert called Dendain—where it will remain until the Day of Judgment, when it will finally be slain.

But what is Behemoth? Said to be 7 miles (11 km) in length, this unidentified creature is described in great detail in the Old Testament Book of Job: "Behold now Behemoth, which I made with thee; he eateth grass as an ox....He moveth his tail like a cedar: the sinews of his stones are wrapped together. His bones are as strong pieces of brass; his bones are like bars of iron....Surely the mountains bring him forth food, where all the beasts of the field play. He lieth under the shady trees, in the covert of the reed, and fens. The shady trees cover him with their shadow; the willows of the brook compass him about. Behold, he drinketh up a river, and hasteth not: he trusteth that he can draw up Jordan into his mouth."

Traditionally, Behemoth is deemed to be either a hippopotamus or a crocodile. Yet neither of these fits the description very satisfactorily. After all, Behemoth's ability to move his tail "like a cedar" implies a long, powerful appendage—a far cry from the hippo's short, insignificant tail. And a vegetarian crocodile—one that "eateth grass as an ox"—would be a rare beast indeed.

American biologist Professor Roy Mackal has boldly stated that, in his opinion, Behemoth might be an undiscovered species of living long-necked dinosaur, similar to *Diplodocus* and *Apatosaurus*. Such a beast would certainly resemble the Bible's description of Behemoth (*see also pp.72–73*).

How fascinating, and how sensational, it would be if a dragon of the past proves to be a dinosaur of the future.

Serpent Dragons and Serpent Whales

Leviathan may not be the only type of serpent dragon inspired by sightings of real creatures that still elude official scientific discovery.

Many aquatic serpent dragons, especially those that could allegedly throw their sinuous bodies into a series of vertical loops or humps, seem remarkably similar in form to certain mysterious water monsters reported today.

Canada's Lake Okanagan, New Guinea's Lake Dakataua, Lake Flathead in the United States, and the coasts of British Columbia, Scandinavia, and Massachusetts, for instance, are said to harbor such creatures. Their description does not correspond with anything known today; yet it compellingly recalls an unusual type of fish-eating whale, known from paleontological evidence to have existed until at least as recently (geologically speaking) as 25 million years ago.

Such whales, known as zeuglodonts, had only small fins, a flexible neck, and a total length sometimes exceeding 60 feet (18 m). And while true snakes can only flex their bodies into horizontal coils, zeuglodonts could undulate vertically, so corresponding not only with many lake and sea monsters reported in modern times, but also with legends of aquatic serpent dragons.

Zeuglodonts may even have been able to come ashore to mate and give birth, unlike today's whales. If so, while on land, they probably moved by humping their bodies vertically, like giant caterpillars. Tales of great serpent dragons could certainly have been inspired by sightings of such beasts.

The oceans are unimaginably vast and deep, and many large and spectacular species of marine animals are still being discovered. Some of the larger, less-explored rivers and lakes are also revealing sizable and surprising creatures unknown to zoologists. So it would be rash to deny outright the possible persistence of a species of zeuglodont, which could be the origin of some veteran serpent dragons.

An early whale, Basilosaurus, *with its long snakelike body, small head, and undulating motion, may have been the archetypal aquatic serpent dragon.*

Chapter

2

SEMI-DRAGONS

*Lindorms and wyverns fall somewhere
between dragons and serpents. The
two-legged, wingless lindorms have greater
affinities with serpents than with the classical
dragons, while wyverns, which
possess not only a pair of legs but also
a pair of wings, are closer to
the classical dragons.*

THE BRIDE OF THE LINDORM KING

Lindorms were commonly encountered in churchyards, where they devoured human corpses, and they would also sometimes invade churches.

Great numbers of lindorms existed in the mountainous regions of central Europe—indeed, the elaborate, dragon-shaped fountain in Klagenfurt, Austria, was inspired by the discovery in 1335 of a supposed lindorm skull, which later proved to be that of a wooly rhinoceros.

The lindorm's favorite country, however, was Sweden. Here, centuries ago, the queen lay in her bedchamber about to give birth to twins—the fulfillment of many years of empty longing for the children she had seemed destined never to conceive. She smiled as she recalled how she had consulted a soothsayer, who had assured her that in less than a year she would be granted two handsome sons, provided that she ate two fresh onions as soon as she returned to the palace.

Although this advice had seemed quite bizarre, the queen had been so aroused by the chance it offered her that she had rushed away, ignoring the voice of the soothsayer calling after her. Arriving back home, the queen had ordered two crisp onions to be brought to her at once.

The queen was so excited by the promise the onions held that she ate the first one without stopping even to peel the skins from it. Not surprisingly, it tasted disgusting and so, in spite of her enthusiasm, she spent time carefully peeling the second one, stripping away every layer of skin before eating it. Nine months had passed since then, and now, precisely as foretold by the soothsayer, her greatly desired sons were about to be born.

Outside the royal bedchamber, the courtiers and palace staff were eagerly awaiting the official announcement of the birth of the new princes. Suddenly, an ear-splitting scream echoed within the chamber. But it was not the lusty cry of a newborn baby; it was, instead, a shriek of horror, a wail that sprang from the throat of the royal midwife when she set eyes upon the queen's first child. It was male—but it was not human.

The queen had given birth to a lindorm, a hideous, snakelike dragon, whose wingless body thrashed upon the marble floor in scaly coils, and from whose shoulders sprang a pair of powerful limbs with taloned feet. So repulsed by the creature that she was unable even to whisper, let alone scream, the queen leaned down, took the

A splendid lindorm depicted in the alchemical scrolls of Sir George Ripley, who lived in England in the 15th century.

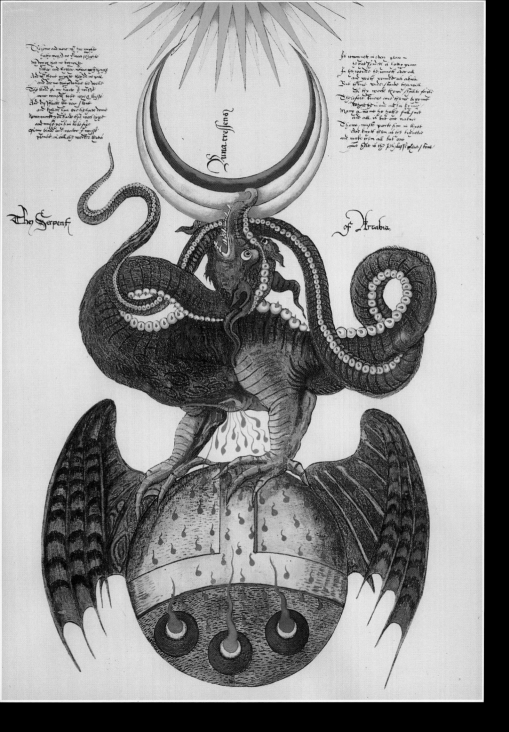

Luna crescens

The Serpent

of Arabia

young lindorm in her hands and hurled it through the window into the dense forest surrounding the palace. Weakened from the exertion, the queen sank back upon the bed and gave birth again, this time to a perfectly healthy, fresh-faced boy, with golden hair and sparkling blue eyes.

Years passed, and the boy became a youthful prince in search of a bride, but what he found was his brother, the lindorm. The prince was riding around the edge of the vast forest encompassing the palace when, without warning, a huge head emerged from a thorny bush directly in front of him. Rearing up until its green-scaled body resembled a towering tree, the lindorm gazed down at the youth with unblinking amber eyes that penetrated his innermost thoughts. And as the prince stared back, mesmerized and motionless, he heard its voice assuring him with cold, reptilian detachment and certainty that he would never find a wife until he, the elder brother, had obtained the true love of a willing bride.

Accordingly, over the next few months a succession of village maidens was given to the lindorm in the hope of overcoming this barrier to the young prince's quest for a bride. Needless to say, none of the maidens came willingly, however, and so none was accepted by the monster. The situation seemed irredeemable, until the next maiden selected to be the bride of the lindorm had the good fortune to encounter the same soothsayer whom

An heraldic device on the main gate of the Physic Garden in London depicts the sun god with the lunar dragon, which resembles a lindorm.

the queen had consulted so many years before. After listening while the maiden spoke of her impending plight, the soothsayer whispered into her ear a few words that swiftly replaced her sadness with a smile of delight.

That night, the maiden was presented to the lindorm, who gruffly told her to take off her dresses, of which she seemed to be wearing a surprising number. She agreed to do this, but only after extracting from the lindorm the promise that for every dress she took off, it would shed a layer of skin. This it did, until only one remained, and until the maiden was clothed in just a single simple garment.

Despite remembering the soothsayer's words, it was not without nervousness that she removed this final gown and stood naked before the great dragon. The lindorm moved toward her, and the maiden tensed—fearing, yet also desiring, what

was to come, for if the soothsayer had spoken truthfully there would be great happiness and great love ahead. And so she stood erect and motionless as the serpentine monster leisurely, almost tenderly, enveloped her body in its scaly coils. She had expected them to feel cold and slimy, but was pleasantly surprised by their warmth and softness when they embraced and caressed her. Even so, she felt a flicker of terror rising within her and a desire to flee. Then the words of the soothsayer came back into her mind, calming her, and she relaxed again.

Gazing about, she noticed that the lindorm's last layer of skin, so thin as to be almost translucent, was starting to peel away, folding back upon itself like a cluster of withered leaves. At the same time, a strange green mist manifested itself, enveloping the lindorm, until she was aware of its presence only by the embrace of its sinuous body. Gradually the mist dispersed and revealed that she was no longer wrapped within the serpentine coils of a lindorm, but held in the firm arms of the most handsome man she had ever seen.

The soothsayer had indeed spoken truthfully. By following her instructions, the maiden had dispelled the enchantment that had incarcerated him within the body of a lindorm, and here was the elder prince, heir to the throne, for whom she would certainly be a willing bride.

The joyful marriage took place without delay, and after the old queen had given her blessing to

In this woodcut from a book of fairy tales, the lindorm tenderly watches the maiden remove her dress, while at her feet lies the first of his many skins.

the newlyweds, now the king and queen, she felt a light tap on her shoulder. It was the soothsayer, who revealed the information the queen had not stayed to hear all those years ago—to be sure to peel both onions before eating them.

Siegfried and the
Slaying of Fafnir

*Several years after the death of Sigmund, last
in the ancient Hun lineage of the Volsung
warrior kings, his widow Queen Hjordis
married King Alf of Denmark.*

He was a good man who loved his stepson
Siegfried as much as his own sons—perhaps even
more, for Siegfried alone possessed the courageous bearing of a Viking king, which made it all
the more ironic that he could never succeed to
Alf's throne.

Someone else, however, recognized the heroic
promise displayed by Siegfried—the dwarf Regin,
who for many years had lived at Alf's court,
teaching the mysterious skills of metal-shaping,
rune-casting, and herbal healing. And Regin's
cunning mind began to weave a web of deception
into which he would entice this unsuspecting
youth. For if a certain dragon could be slain,
Regin stood to gain immense wealth and power,
and of all mortals only Siegfried seemed capable
of accomplishing such a deed.

One day, with studied innocence, Regin
remarked to Siegfried how sad it was that, while
all his stepbrothers were assured of position and
respect as heirs to their father's dominion, he had
nothing comparable to look forward to. Unless,
that is, he decided to seek fame as a fearless
warrior, in the tradition of his Volsung forefathers.

Siegfried was readily persuaded by the appeal
of such a notion. And Regin lost no time in telling
him about a terrible dragon called Fafnir, which
frequented a barren realm known as Gnitahead
and guarded a vast hoard of treasure. To slay such
a monster would gain Siegfried great honor and
esteem. Feigning disinterest in the treasure, Regin
promised that if Siegfried were to venture upon
this daring quest, he would accompany him and
would offer whatever advice he could for killing
the fearful creature.

Many years before, Siegfried's mother had
presented him with the broken halves of his
father's wondrous, gleaming sword, Gram, and
Regin made Siegfried a further promise—to forge
the two halves of his father's blade into a new,
whole sword that would guarantee a successful
outcome in his confrontation with the dragon. As
Regin had anticipated, his pledge to restore Gram
was, in itself, sufficiently alluring to gain
Siegfried's interest, and not long afterward the
two were riding through the lonely heathland that
led to the stronghold of their quarry.

*In 1880, Konrad Dielitz portrayed Siegfried, in
the spirit of medieval legend, as a courageous
and romantic truly Nordic hero doing battle
with a huge and formidable foe.*

Siegfried knew Regin well enough to deduce that the dwarf's interest in the quest probably stemmed from avarice, but he could hardly have begun to suspect the dark history and dire treachery that encapsulated quest and treasure alike.

Dwarves are ancient beings for whom millennia pass almost unnoticed in their shadowy subterranean kingdoms. Countless years before the birth of Siegfried, a miserly dwarf king had been cut down by one of his own sons, who coveted the king's vast cache of gold and gems. That son was Fafnir, and Fafnir's brother was Regin.

After gaining his father's wealth, Fafnir retreated with it to Gnitahead and jealously guarded it. But the treasure was tainted by his dying father's curse, and its evil influence, enhanced by his own corrupt nature, wrought a terrible transformation in Fafnir. He gloated over the hoard with the lust of a dragon, so ultimately, he became one, metamorphosing into a huge and terrible lindorm, whose great claws caressed the

The Siegfried story has always had a strong appeal in Germany; Richard Wagner wrote an opera based on it, and this still is from The Niebelung, *a two-part film made by Fritz Lang in 1922–24.*

cold, glittering coins and jewels that lay in heaps on every side, and whose serpentine body enfolded them within its scaly, scintillating coils.

For centuries, dreams of this treasure had festered in Regin's mind. He had craved a chance to make it his own and now, at last, with Siegfried as his unwitting pawn, that opportunity had arrived. Once Fafnir had been slain, his wealth would be Regin's, as would a magical power even more secret and more precious, after which Siegfried would no longer be required. A smile, as dark and chilling as his thoughts, flickered like a serpent's tongue across Regin's face as he rode in Siegfried's wake toward Fafnir's cave.

When they reached the cave mouth, the dragon was nowhere to be seen, for this was the time when he took his daily drink from a nearby stream. Fafnir's magnificent scaling rendered him virtually impregnable to weapons; only his naked belly was vulnerable, so this was where the fatal blow must be delivered. Following Regin's advice, Siegfried dug a deep pit in the path along which Fafnir would return and hid in it, while Regin disguised the opening with branches.

Hours crawled by like eons for Siegfried as he lay in the pit, silent and ready. Then suddenly, a loud swishing noise reached his ears; something immensely large and heavy was slithering along the path toward his hiding place. It was Fafnir.

Siegfried held the hilt of Gram firmly in both hands and raised its shining, lethal blade vertically, until the tip was directly below the concealed opening. No sooner had he done so than a pair of huge reptilian limbs straddled the pit as the massive lindorm began to move across it, exposing his unprotected belly. Siegfried thrust Gram upward with all his might and felt its blade plunge into Fafnir's torso. It was a deep, mortal wound that called forth a single shriek of pain from the dragon before his corpse crashed to the ground.

Scarcely had Siegfried clambered out of the pit and retrieved his sword than Regin appeared, his eyes glittering with delight. Without a word, he took his own weapon, a short dagger hewn from some mysterious metal, and, with its sharp

A carving in the 12th-century church at Hylestad, Norway, depicts Siegfried, crouched in the pit, thrusting his sword into Fafnir.

point, hooked out the lindorm's heart. Turning to Siegfried, he bade him light a fire, roast the heart in it, and give it to him to eat. Regin alleged that this was merely a symbolic gesture, and despite his earlier suspicions, the youth saw no reason to doubt him; Regin had, after all, kept his word throughout their quest.

Siegfried did as he was bidden, but just before handing the heart to the dwarf he touched it with a finger to test whether it was fully cooked. The hot flesh burned him, so to soothe the pain Siegfried licked his finger and instantly heard chattering voices overhead. Puzzled, he looked up, and to his amazement discovered that the voices were those of birds in a tree above him. Tasting the heart of Fafnir had given him the power to understand the speech of animals. But as he listened, astonishment gave way to alarm, for the birds were discussing how, even as they spoke, Regin was plotting Siegfried's murder.

Enraged, the youth ran to Regin, and when he looked into the dwarf's malevolent eyes, he saw only too plainly the truth of the birds' words, and the deceit of Regin's. Moments later, Gram claimed a second victim, and Regin's head rolled down the path to lie alongside the carcass of his brother Fafnir. Siegfried, meanwhile, walked into the cave to claim the treasure and, unbeknown to him, the curse that accompanied it.

Maud and the Wyvern

The image of the wyvern is as manifold as it is manifest, and few dragons are so intimately associated with symbolism as the wyvern.

It appears as the emblem of envy, insignia of war, personification of pestilence, representation of non-transmuted matter in alchemy, disguise of the devil, and as a prevalent device in heraldry. Rarely, however, does it elicit emotions of friendship or love—which is why the medieval legend of the Mordiford wyvern is so unexpectedly poignant.

Maud's parents had little objection to their young daughter owning a cat or dog—but they were more than a little perturbed by the creature that stood before them, small and colorful though it might be. Earlier that day, Maud had been walking through the woods near her home at Mordiford, in the English county of Herefordshire, when she came upon a strange little animal looking forlorn and dejected. It was poking its snout listlessly into a clump of flowers and was quite evidently lost.

The creature looked like a baby dragon: its body was no bigger than a cucumber and

Leonardo da Vinci's drawing of a dragon attacking a lion shows an immense and terrifying wyvern.

its bright green scales—sparkling like shining peridots in the sunlight—made it appear even more like one as it squatted upon its single pair of legs. Every so often, it would open its fragile, membranous wings and flutter them hopefully, but it was clearly far too young to fly. As soon as it saw Maud, however, its sadness evaporated, and it began chasing merrily around her, frolicking with joy that it was no longer alone.

Maud was thoroughly enchanted by her unexpected playmate and happily took it back home with her, convinced that her parents would share her delight in the tiny creature. But they recognized it as a wyvern (albeit a very young one), and their reaction was very different. In words that brooked no opposition,

*St. Michael and the angels are depicted fighting Satan in the guise of a wyvern in the **Liber Floridus**, a Flemish manuscript dating from 1448.*

they insisted that she should take it back to where she had found it and leave it there. Steeling themselves to ignore her tearful protestations, they closed the cottage door behind her and watched, sadly but with great relief, as their daughter walked slowly back to the woods, followed by her strange little companion.

Once out of their sight, however, Maud turned away from the main woodland path and ran instead toward her secret hiding place—a little nook known only to her, where she spent many happy hours concealed from the rest of the world. Here she placed her new-found pet, and here it would remain, where she could visit it, play with it, and feed it every day, safe from the prying eyes of her parents and the other Mordiford folk.

As the months went by, however, Maud's pet grew ever larger, and at a quite alarming rate. The cucumberlike youngster was maturing into an impressive adult wyvern, whose soft green scales had hardened into razor-sharp disks of a deep viridescent tone, whose gossamer wings had become leathery and bat-like, and whose curly tail now bore at its tip a deadly sting.

The saucers of milk brought to it each day by the ever-faithful Maud, which had once satisfied its juvenile appetite, were no longer able to dispel

A painting of the wyvern could be seen on the wall of Mordiford church until c.1811, when, despite pleas from the villagers, it was destroyed by the vicar, who believed it unseemly for the symbol of the devil to be displayed there.

her pet's pangs of ravenous hunger. And so it began to seek sustenance elsewhere. The local farming community soon suffered great losses of livestock, and it was not long before the culprit was unmasked. Maud's dragon had acquired a liking for the flesh of sheep and cows. But worse was to come. When some of the bolder farmers attempted to deal with the monster, it ably defended itself, and in so doing discovered another taste much to its liking—humans!

Maud was devastated by the actions of her former playmate and begged it to end its murderous assaults upon the townsfolk, but to no avail. Not even gentle rearing by a loving child could suppress indefinitely the irascible nature and predatory instincts of a true dragon. With the advent of maturity, these had inevitably been unleashed in a violent torrent of uncontrollable, primeval force. Just one person remained safe from the marauding wyvern—Maud, its early playmate and friend.

Not for her the flame and the fear, only the love that even the heart of the most terrible dragon contains, but which is so rarely ignited by humans. She alone could walk safely beside it, stroke its ebony claws, and gaze without trepidation into its eyes of blazing chrysolite. Such is the power of friendship and love.

Instinctively raising his shield, Garston deflected the great blast of fire that roared from the wyvern's gaping jaws and aimed his lance at its throat, distended from the force of its expulsion of flame. The lance pierced the monster's flesh, and an explosion of dark blood burst forth, staining the grass.

Garston also carried a sharp sword, and was about to plunge it into the stricken creature's head when a young girl, screaming not in fear but in hysterical rage, ran out of some bushes and started hurling stones at him. His horse reared up in alarm, but far more startling to Garston was the extraordinary sight of this same child, kneeling on the blood-soaked grass and weeping uncontrollably, with her arms around the neck of the dying wyvern.

Unnerved, and oddly perturbed by his success in slaying the huge dragon that had terrorized Mordiford for so long, Garston rode away, back to the joyful villagers—leaving behind a dead monster with its only friend, a girl called Maud for whom the innocence of childhood had come to a sudden and savagely premature end.

Neither of these, however, was enough to change the inevitable course that events were about to take. The wyvern's tyranny had to be countered if Mordiford's inhabitants were to survive. And so it was that one morning, a tall figure encased in armor and mounted upon a magnificent steed rode into the woods, with a sturdy lance grasped firmly in his hand.

A member of Mordiford's most illustrious family, the Garstons, he dismounted and courageously sought out his dreadful quarry. Suddenly, from amid a tangled mass of foliage, a massive green monster lunged forward; its scaly covering had imitated so intimately the leafy vegetation that it had been completely invisible as it lay in wait for its opponent.

Marduk and the Sea Dragon

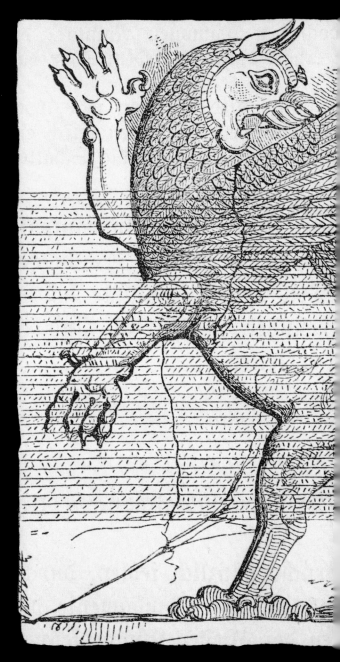

According to Assyro-Babylonian mythology, at the beginning of the world there were two primordial beings—Apsu, the male incarnation of fresh water and space; and Tiamat, the female incarnation of the sea and chaos.

From these descended a great and varied dynasty of gods. At first they lived in harmony with their ancestors, but as their numbers increased and their voices grew bolder, the new gods began to challenge the ancient order established by Apsu.

Ultimately, Apsu became so incensed by their irreverence that he and a somewhat reluctant Tiamat plotted their progeny's destruction, but they were overheard. Alerted, the gods acted swiftly, seizing Apsu and slaying him. Until then, Tiamat had sought to temper Apsu's evil intent, to lighten his mood and dispel his hatred for their descendants; but when she learned that they had killed him, her erstwhile love for them transformed into a hatred even more potent than that of Apsu—an unquenchable thirst for vengeance that she furiously channeled into the creation of a vast army of monstrous acolytes.

Men with the scaly tails of fishes or the poisonous stings of scorpions, great serpents with coils of constricting death, hideous hounds with blazing eyes of fire, sentient storms, all were conjured up by her vitriolic wrath. Swelling their

An engraving of Marduk, the ancient Assyrian sun god, fighting a dragon; copied from a relief at Nimrud and reproduced in A.H. Layard's book Nineveh and Babylon. *The monster is portrayed not as the elongated sea dragon Tiamat, but as a griffinlike beast.*

ranks were several gods who pledged loyalty to her rather than to their fellow immortals.

And to set the seal upon what she believed to be an inevitable triumph, Tiamat transformed herself into a terrifying semi-dragon—a serpentine horror with impervious scales, two powerful muscular forelegs whose feet were equipped with daggerlike talons, a long neck held proudly erect, and a pair of curved horns upon her head.

At first, the other gods were appalled. Who could stand against such an onslaught of animate nightmares? After much deliberation, however, the valiant sun god Marduk agreed to do battle single-handedly with Tiamat and her macabre entourage, provided that he was accepted forever afterward as the supreme god. Not surprisingly, eliciting this promise from his brethren proved an easy task, infinitely easier than the one that he now undertook.

Undaunted, Marduk set forth to confront his terrible foe. He armed himself with an immense net in which he planned to capture Tiamat, a bow and arrows with which he hoped to slay her, and, most crucial of all to his strategy, the allegiance of the untamable hurricane. Transported by the power of a tumultuous, raging tempest, he swiftly reached the appointed battlefield, and at once the massed forces of Tiamat arose to destroy him.

But as Tiamat approached, with her troops in her wake, Marduk flung his net over this vast monster, enveloping her in an inextricable tangle of mesh that bound her so tightly she was unable to break free. Immediately, Marduk directed the wild fury of the hurricane into her face, and, as expected, Tiamat opened her colossal jaws in a frenzied attempt to engulf her persecutor. The hurricane surged into her mouth, exerting the full force of its raging power to prevent her from closing her jaws again, gripping her heart with chill fingers of ice and inflating her belly with its vigorous breath.

In that same moment, Marduk directed an arrow, straight and true, between Tiamat's gaping jaws into her unprotected belly, where its deadly head tore through her flesh. Losing no time, Marduk sliced apart her internal organs, split her heart into two, and continued to assail her prostrate form until Tiamat, the embodiment of chaos, was no more. Only then did he cease his attack, to stand proudly erect upon her corpse—wordlessly conveying to all that he, Marduk, was the victor, and that he, Marduk, was now the supreme power.

The head of a dragon, the symbol of Marduk, sculpted in bronze and dating from c.800–600 B.C., was found in Mesopotamia and is now in the Louvre Museum, Paris.

Ancient Babylonian cylinder seals were sometimes signet rings, but more often they were barrel-shaped objects made from baked clay and engraved with writing or with a picture. When the seal was rolled along wax, it left an impression—here it is of Marduk pursuing Tiamat.

The old order was no more. Once he had annihilated all her panic-stricken followers, too, Marduk set about creating an entire world from the carcass of Tiamat. After cleaving her body in two, he fashioned one half into the heavens, and molded the other into the earth. He set the stars in the heavens and garnished the earth with fields, forests, rivers, and mountains, populating them with a teeming myriad of wildlife.

Last, from the crimson torrent gushing out of the veins of Kingu, one of Tiamat's slain supporters, Marduk created humankind, a race born from blood and destined to spill so much of its own in the ages to come.

Tiamat has been linked with another monster, the lamia. According to the Swiss analytical psychologist Carl Jung, lamia is the name of a huge, marine fishlike monster, and the word "lamia" comes from the Greek *lamos*, meaning abyss—all of which implies a kinship with the sea dragon, Tiamat.

However, the lamia is more often portrayed as a scaly four-legged beast with a woman's face and breasts. It has also been described as a shape-shifting serpent, which assumes the guise of a voluptuous maiden who drains away the blood, and the life, of any man unlucky enough to be seduced by its deadly wiles.

Fortunately, there is a simple way of distinguishing a lamia from a real woman. Although it has a musical voice, it cannot speak; when it attempts to do so, all that emerges is a terrible hissing sound and a slender forked tongue, which betray its true nature.

THE ELUSIVE TATZELWORM

For centuries, people living in the Bavarian, Austrian, and Swiss Alps have claimed that the mountains are the home of an extraordinary animal known locally as the tatzelworm.

This "clawed worm," also called the *Stollenwurm,* or hole-dwelling worm, is said to be a snakelike reptilian beast 4–5 feet (1.2–1.5 m) long, with two clearly visible forelegs (only very occasionally have hind legs been reported)—in short, a mysterious creature wholly unlike any species known by science to exist in this part of the world, and bearing more than a passing resemblance to a lindorm.

Some reports describe its head as catlike, and it is supposedly capable of jumping considerable distances. One day in the summer of 1921, at Hochfilzen in southern Austria, a feline-headed tatzelworm allegedly leaped at a herdsman and a poacher, who had ill-advisedly taken a shot at it; both men promptly fled in terror.

Although these remarkable animals have been reported many times before and since and, according to local lore, have even been killed on rare occasions, zoologists have yet to receive the body of one for identification.

In 1954, Sicilian farmers reported that a creature with a cat's head and a serpent's body had attacked their pigs; could it have been a tatzelworm?

Similar creatures have been seen farther south, too. One of the most famous modern-day records dates from 1954, when a number of farmers claimed to have spied a cat-headed snakelike beast with two legs attacking a herd of pigs near Palermo in Sicily.

Those zoologists willing to believe in the tatzelworm's reality have suggested that it could be a large, undiscovered skink, or lizard, for some of them have elongated bodies but only very small limbs. Others have proposed that it is not a reptile but a siren, an eel-like amphibian without hind legs; sirens are, however, known to exist only in North America.

As discussed elsewhere in this book, several types of dragon may well have been inspired by sightings of living animals. Perhaps, therefore, the lindorm (many tales of which stem from central Europe) is also based upon a real creature, but one that continues to elude formal scientific discovery.

Chapter

3

CLASSICAL DRAGONS

*The classical Western dragon extensively
depicted in heraldry is the ferocious, fire-emitting
reptilian nemesis of countless heroes from
mythological and medieval times. This
monstrous beast was encased in an impenetrable
armor of scintillating scales and borne upon
four powerful limbs with talon-tipped feet.
It wielded a long sweeping tail, terminating in
an arrow-headed sting; and often, but not
invariably, sported a pair of huge, batlike wings.*

St. George and the Dragon

*As the third century dawned, so, too, did the day the king
of Silene, in Libya, had been awaiting with dread.
For on that morning, his beloved daughter
was to be sacrificed to the monster that had been
terrorizing his land for what seemed like an eternity.*

This beast—a huge, winged dragon, with a long, spiraling tail and olive-green, crocodilian scales—had emerged from Silene's vast swamplands many months before and had choked the countryside with evil-smelling clouds of poisonous vapor that blighted everything it enveloped.

In an attempt to end its violation of their fields, local farmers had fed the monster with two sheep each day. This strategy had succeeded until the time came when there were no more sheep, whereupon the reptilian tyrant recommenced its own campaign of devastation by asphyxiation. That was when, with a heavy heart, the wretched king had finally agreed to the daily sacrifice of a child, in the hope of assuaging the dragon's appetite long enough for some miracle to deliver his country from this abomination.

In Vittore Carpaccio's evocative painting dating from c.1502, St. George skewers a typical four-legged classical dragon, but in this version, the dragon's wings are eyeless.

God's hand can be seen blessing St. George, who is the patron saint of Barcelona, in this altar panel painted c.1410 by the Spanish artist Mazel de Sas.

The princess had been standing bound upright to the stake for only a few minutes when her face grew ashen with fear, for she heard a thunderous tread approaching ever nearer—surely the herald of her impending doom. But suddenly she realized that the sounds were coming not from the swamp ahead but from the plains directly behind her.

She craned her neck to find out what, or who, was causing them and saw a tall knight, clad in silver-gray armor, with a white breastplate upon which was emblazoned a scarlet cross. He had just dismounted from a cream-coated charger and was carrying a long lance and white shield, once again adorned with a cross of scarlet, as he strode toward the tethered maiden.

The princess lost no time in explaining her terrible situation to the knight, and he, in turn, quickly told her about himself. His name was George, he had grown up in eastern Turkey, in Cappadocia, and had been a soldier in the Roman army before becoming converted to Christianity. Now he served no one but God, spreading the Lord's word wherever he journeyed.

A corporeal manifestation of evil, the dragon embodied everything that George had pledged to confront and conquer—and so, heedless of her pleas to save himself while there was still time, George untied the princess and stood in her stead, valiantly prepared for battle with her monstrous foe. He did not have to wait long. Without warning, the dense reed beds fronting a steaming quagmire close by were thrust apart, as

But the days, and the weeks, had fled by, and no miracle had occurred. And at last the morning had arrived when it was the turn of the king's own daughter, the fair princess Alcyone, to be tied to a wooden stake at the edge of the swamp and surrendered to the loathsome creature. No one suspected that the miracle for which the king and everyone else in Silene had prayed so earnestly and for so long was about to take place.

a great reptilian head, borne upon a powerful neck, forced its way through them. It was followed by a massive body supported on four muscular limbs and with a lithe tail twisting furiously like a corkscrew.

During the course of his travels through many strange lands, George had seen all manner of vile, misbegotten apparitions, but nothing prepared him for the wave of revulsion that swept over him as he beheld the dragon of Silene. Dripping with stinking slime that only emphasized the livid hue of its scales, the hideous creature resembled a huge mound of rotting meat— green with putrefaction, oozing decay, and reeking of death.

Longing to avert his eyes and his nose from such a sickening presence, but intent upon banishing the monster from the face of the earth, George raised his right arm—and was about to plunge his lance into the dragon's throat, when two shapeless lumps flanking the broad base of its neck suddenly burst into life.

To his bewilderment, George found himself surrounded by a flurry of blazing eyes. Everywhere he looked, they glowed and dazzled him, hypnotizing him with their terrible allure, until he raised his arm again and hurled the lance with all his might into the midst of these spell-binding,

In the early 19th century, prints were often sold with a separate metallic sheet, which was then cut up and stuck to parts of the print to create a tinsel picture. In this example, George has even been given a real feather as a helmet plume.

unblinking orbs. A terrible scream rent the air, and the eyes suddenly vanished.

No longer mesmerized by their movement, the knight looked down, and there lay the dragon, still alive but mortally wounded, his great lance through its throat and protruding out of the back of its neck. And over its prone body, like an ornate shroud, lay its immense wings, whose bright markings, resembling an array of brilliant eyes, had so bewitched his vision.

Running to him in delight came the princess Alcyone, and once they had tied the girdle of her robe around the subdued dragon's neck, they rode back to her father's castle, leading the monster alongside George's mighty steed. There, in return for the knight's promise to slay the dragon, the joyful king of Silene and his subjects willingly agreed to be baptized and converted to the Christian faith. True to his word, George beheaded their one-time oppressor and, after bidding farewell to the grateful Alcyone, her deliverer rode away, into a future that would shortly transform him into a Christian martyr.

Many centuries later, he was adopted by an army of medieval crusaders as the patron saint of their nation—and in this way became known as St. George of England.

The Embarrassing Exit of the Wantley Dragon

*In the time of Elizabeth I of England, outside
the Yorkshire village of Wortley, in a lodge called
Wantley, there lived a dreadful dragon.*

It had a predilection for trampling the trees, munching the milk cows, and generally pestering the populace. In despair, the villagers approached More of More Hall, a famously virile local knight, begging him to rid them of this irksome menace.

More agreed to do what he could, but only if, on the evening before the battle, a fair-skinned, dark-haired damsel was presented to him, to perform the duties of anointing his body with oil and dressing him the next morning. While every fair-skinned, dark-haired damsel in the area attempted to persuade the village elders that she should be chosen for this important task, More traveled to Sheffield, where he commissioned an expert armorer to create a suit bristling with spikes of steel 6 inches (15 cm) long. Later, More returned to Wantley wearing his porcupine mail, and retired to his hall, eager to meet his maidenly attendant and to locate the jar of anointing oil.

Although he did not emerge until a disgracefully late hour, More seemed surprisingly weary the following morning. So to fortify and invigorate him, the villagers supplied him with six pots of ale, which he quaffed thirstily before setting out in search of the dragon. Knowing that his reptilian foe regularly drank at a certain well, More cunningly crept inside it and, when the dragon arrived, leaped out and smote him heavily upon the jaw. Due no doubt to the potent mixture of fright and fury generated by such a sneaky attack, the aggrieved animal defecated exuberantly in the knight's direction.

More at once engaged the dragon in battle, but two-and-a-half days later, the combatants had failed to inflict a single wound upon one another. More's spiny suit rendered him invulnerable, and the dragon's great scalloped scales were similarly impregnable. Finally, More grasped the dragon and hauled it around until its head and forequarters faced directly away from him. He had been informed by the villagers that the monster had only one vulnerable spot, and there was only one way to test their claim. He raised his right foot, encased in a sharply pointed steel boot, took careful aim, and then kicked the unsuspecting dragon with all his might.

With a shriek of pain and embarrassment, the dragon leaped into the air, turning six times before collapsing on the ground. For a few moments, it lay quaking and rumbling, but after a final emanation of dung the monster expired, and More returned in triumph to his raven-haired attendant—and a new jar of anointing oil.

More takes a well-aimed kick at the Wantley dragon's only vulnerable spot.

Beware of the Bunyip!

Among the monsters populating
Australia's myths and legends are some
that can certainly claim allegiance
to the dragon dynasty.

The most famous is the bunyip—a freshwater beast of protean potential, for it has been likened by eyewitnesses to a seal, a foal, an emu, a sea cow, a bulldog, and inevitably, a dragon.

Back in the far distant days of Dream Time, the son of the leader of a bold warrior tribe set out one day to seek a gift with which to win the favor of a maiden. Nothing commonplace would suffice; hours passed and still he had not found anything that satisfied him, until he came to a large pool in which an amazing little animal was merrily cavorting. Using his net, the youth soon captured the strange beast, which was unlike anything he had ever seen before.

In shape it recalled a young calf or colt, but its head resembled a bulldog's, with a blunt muzzle and wide jaws brimming with tiny teeth. Its finned tail was long and flattened, its eyes glowed like torches, and its body was tessellated with a mosaic of iridescent scales. Delighted, the youth returned home with this wonderful animal.

However, the tribe's wise leader was horrified. He ordered his son to return it to the pool, for he knew only too well the animal's identity—it was a baby bunyip, and anybody rash enough to abduct one would soon face its mother's terrible wrath.

But already it was too late. A hideous roar like all the summer thunderstorms rolled together echoed across the land, and the fearful people saw that the rivers and lakes had risen, submerging the valleys and plains in an all-embracing flood. In a desperate exodus, the tribe raced up into the mountains, but still the leader's son would not relinquish the little water dragon.

Suddenly, a huge black shadow fell across the fleeing people. It was the mother bunyip, an immense vision of glittering scales, rapacious

THE PIASA, DRAGON BIRD OF ILLINOIS

The monsters that stared down at the Jesuit priest Father Jacques Marquette one day in August 1673 were hideous beyond the wildest, most surrealistic imagination.

How fortunate for him, therefore, that they were merely petroglyphs, painstakingly carved and painted into a cliff face about 80 feet (24 m) above the Mississippi River, along which he was traveling on his passage through Illinois.

According to Father Marquette's Indian guide, these petroglyphs had been created centuries earlier by some long-forgotten ancestral tribe and depicted a terrifying dragon that had once inhabited the region. It was known as the *piasa*, which can be translated as "the bird that devours human beings."

Long ago, the Illini tribe lived in harmony with the piasa, which contented itself by preying upon deer and other large mammals, never molesting the Indians on the plains below the lofty cliff, where it dwelt in an immense cave. Tragically, however, this peaceful equilibrium was destroyed when a warring tribe invaded the Illini's territory. During the ensuing battle, many men from both tribes were killed; and although the Illini eventually triumphed, their success was tempered by an unexpected and thoroughly catastrophic development. Although it had closely observed

The rock paintings of the piasa were destroyed many years ago, and this image, drawn in 1887, was based on legendary descriptions of the dragon bird.

the battle but had not participated in it, for such a rapacious flesh-eater as the piasa, the presence of so many newly dead bodies was far too tempting to be ignored.

Never before had the piasa tasted the flesh of humans, but to its surprise and delight, it discovered that this new meat was greatly to its liking. So, from that day onward, the monstrous dragon bird became the mortal enemy of the Illini, regularly swooping down to abduct men, women, and children, bearing them aloft in its great talons and carrying them back to its grim hideaway to be torn apart and devoured. Clearly, if the tribe were to survive, their winged nemesis would have to be vanquished.

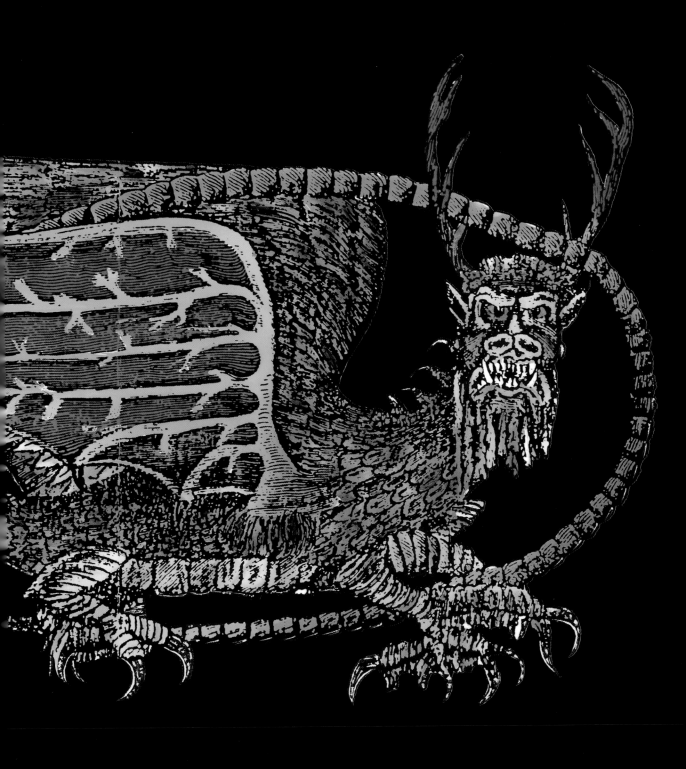

A great meeting was held, attended by every member of the tribe, during which many different plans for getting rid of the piasa were proposed, examined, and ultimately rejected. After several hours of intense discussion, only one strategy had been suggested that offered any real hope for annihilating the tribe's oppressor, and it would be exceedingly hazardous for whoever was chosen as the principal participant in its implementation.

The conference concluded that the most likely means of slaying an airborne monster such as the piasa would be to lure it to the ground, and then for 20 of the tribe's most courageous warriors to ambush it. And the only way of successfully enticing the piasa down from the sky would be to use an effective bait—another warrior, alive but unarmed.

A brave named Massatoga had proposed this daring strategy after calling upon the Great Spirit for inspiration; and when he volunteered to act as the living bait for the piasa, the tribe decided to implement his plan the following morning. At daybreak, therefore, readily visible to the piasa in its mountainous

A drawing based upon Father Jacques Marquette's description of the discovery of the petroglyph of the piasa on the rocky cliff above the Mississippi near Alton, Illinois.

retreat, Massatoga stood by the Mississippi River, raised his arms to the skies, and began to chant in a loud, clear voice, calling upon the Great Spirit for assistance in overcoming the tribe's aerial persecutor. Suddenly, as his strong voice continued to echo across the rolling plains, the sky overhead grew dark, although there was not a cloud in sight. It was the piasa.

The dragon bird descended rapidly, and even the valiant Massatoga felt his heart quake with fear as his horrific foe came into view. As red as blood, as black as night, as green as bile, this tricolored apparition was at least 30 feet (9 m) long and around 12 feet (4 m) tall, and it sported a mighty pair of leathery wings, with a span of 16–18 feet (5–5.5 m).

Its entire body and all four of its legs were covered in scales, and each of its feet was armed with a cluster of black, scimitarlike talons. Lashing through the air as it swept downward was an immensely long, serpentine tail, terminating in a double fin, and its head bore a huge pair of branched antlers like those of a deer.

North American legends contain many monsters, among them dragons such as these, which were attacked by 20 men from the ship Caroline *near New Orleans.*

Even more terrible to Massatoga than any of these was the piasa's face—for it was the face of a man, albeit a grotesque parody of one. Its crimson eyes glowed with infernal malice; from its mouth emerged a spine-chilling shriek of fury. Rows of flesh-ripping teeth lined its jaws; dark vapor swirled out of its broad, apelike nostrils; and a beard of stiff bristles sprouted from its chin.

While still in flight, the piasa extended its talons to grasp Massatoga's body. But he raced toward some nearby trees, pursued by the monster, until the branches forced it to land and fold its wings across its back to prevent them from becoming entangled. Massatoga's companions at once leaped out of their hiding place among the trees, swiftly encompassed the startled dragon bird, and bombarded it with quiver upon quiver of poisoned arrows. Many bounced harmlessly off its scaly hide, but some tore its wings, preventing it from taking flight, and others pierced its face.

Blinded and wounded by the onslaught, the piasa was unable to protect itself as the warriors clambered upon its mighty body and began hacking through its flesh with their sharp knives and tomahawks. Soon the once-feared monster was no more.

Sadly, the same is also true of the splendid petroglyphs spied by Father Marquette. In or around 1856, some quarry work close by disrupted the cliff face, shattering its unique artwork, which crumbled and cascaded into the river. The passing of the piasa was complete.

THE SIRRUSH OF BABYLON

One of the greatest archaeological events of the twentieth century was the disinterment of ancient Babylon's magnificent Ishtar Gate.

Excavations began in 1899, and for three years the German archaeologist Professor Robert Koldewey labored to uncover this spectacular edifice dedicated to the sun god Marduk. The gateway was erected during the reign of King Nebuchadnezzar II (605–562 B.C.) to lead visitors in breathtaking fashion into the religious center of Babylon. But after the city's fall *c.*39 B.C., it was buried beneath the Mesopotamian sands and forgotten by the world until its resurrection by Koldewey's team. Theirs were the first modern eyes to behold its dazzling panoply of highly glazed cobalt-colored bricks and horizontal rows of animals represented in realistic bas-relief.

Three types of animals were present: a bull, a lion, and a dragon. The first two were clearly inspired by living animals, but what about the dragon? Even though it was portrayed just as realistically as the bull and the lion, it was surely a wholly mythical, imaginary beast—or was it? The sacred animal of Marduk, Babylon's dragon was

Dragons, based perhaps on a living dinosaur, were among the animals on the gate spanning the processional way between the temples of

known as the *sirrush*, or *mushussu*, and Koldewey was far from convinced that it was nothing more than a fabulous creature of legend. Although Babylonian depictions of all other fabulous beasts had changed dramatically over the centuries, those of the sirrush had always remained the same, like those of the real animals.

Yet if the sirrush were indeed based upon a living creature, what could it be? With a slender four-legged body covered in fine scales, powerful clawed feet, a long neck, lengthy tail, and a horn upon its head (possibly representing a pair, since the sirrush was depicted in profile), it was visibly different from anything known in modern times. So Koldewey conceived the fascinating notion that this dragonesque beast might have been modeled on an undiscovered living dinosaur.

Many present-day zoologists acknowledge that depictions of the sirrush do resemble a somewhat distorted portrait of certain reptilian giants from the prehistoric world, particularly those long-necked herbivorous dinosaurs known as sauropods, which are typified by such familiar creatures as *Diplodocus* and *Apatosaurus* (formerly called *Brontosaurus*).

In addition, discrepancies of form between the sirrush and sauropods could be readily explained if the artists responsible for the depictions were working not from direct, personal observations of living dinosaurs, but merely from secondhand descriptions by travelers or other eyewitnesses. If, therefore, some 65 million years after the dinosaurs' official extinction, the sauropod lineage does indeed still exist, eluding formal scientific discovery yet seemingly known to the ancient Babylonians, where should we look for these living wonders?

Not long after the Ishtar Gate's re-emergence, the explorer Hans Schomburgk returned to Europe from Central Africa with a glazed brick

A beast like a dinosaur, known to local people as the mokele-mbembe, *is supposed still to exist in the Likouala swamps of the Congo. This huge creature may have been the inspiration for the Babylonian sirrush.*

that he had found there, a brick exactly like those in the Ishtar Gate. If this was where they had been obtained by the Babylonian builders, the find is particularly intriguing because Schomburgk also brought back amazing reports of mysterious dinosaur-like beasts.

These were said to resemble *Apatosaurus*, and to inhabit Central Africa's vast, virtually inaccessible swamp-lands. Was this merely a coincidence, or were these beasts seen by the Babylonians and incorporated into their art as the sirrush?

The most famous of the possible living dino-saurs in tropical Africa is an elusive water crea-ture, the *mokele-mbembe*, which is supposed to inhabit the huge Likouala swamps in the People's Republic of the Congo. In the past 200 years alone, many local and European observers have spied it, and during the 1980s several expeditions (notably those led by the biologist Professor Roy Mackal of Chicago University) trekked through these swamps in the hope of confirming its existence.

According to eyewitness testimony, the *mokele-mbembe* has a large elephantine body, a long slender neck and small head, four massive limbs, and clawed feet that leave distinctive three-toed

The dragon in the temple of Bel may have been a mokele-mbembe. *If so, Daniel was probably the only person in the civilized world to have killed a dinosaur.*

prints. A hefty tapering tail and a total length of about 30 feet (9 m) complete a compelling des-cription of a small sauropod dinosaur. Even the three-toed footprints, which do not match those of any animal known in that area, are typical of certain sauropods. Simi-larly, drawings of the beast by local observers readily recall a sauro-pod, and when shown pictures of living and prehistoric animals, the locals have consistently identified sauropods as the *mokele-mbembe*.

There is, however, an even more startling aspect to this tanta-lizing case. The biblical Apocrypha tells a story of a dragon, living in the temple of the Babylonian deity Bel, that was worshipped as a god, and which Daniel choked to death to demon-strate that it was mortal, like any other beast. There has been much controversy among biblical scholars as to whether this dragon really existed, and, if it did, what it could have been. In view of the thought-provoking link between the sirrush and the Congo's mysterious water beast, some zoologists have proposed that it could have been a living *mokele-mbembe*, captured in Central Africa, possibly while still a juvenile, and transported alive back to Babylon.

THE DRAGONET OF MOUNT PILATUS

Not all classical dragons were of immense proportions. Some, known as dragonets, were scarcely larger than a man; but despite their smaller size, they were no less deadly.

Typical of these was the dragonet of Mount Pilatus, a creature so inimical that even its blood was instantly lethal to anything it touched. In the Middle Ages, the Swiss town of Wilser was for a long time besieged by this monster, whose fiery breath charred homes, farms, livestock, and people during its frequent forays in search of prey. Yet no one was sufficiently skilled in swordplay to offer any realistic hope of slaying it.

Earlier there had been such a man in Wilser, named Winckelriedt, but his short temper and proficiency with weapons had led to a conviction for manslaughter—whereupon his lands had been seized and he had been banished. Yet it was clear that he alone could free the town from its persecutor, and so Winckelriedt was swiftly recalled. He was told that all charges against him would be dropped and his property restored if he could successfully dispatch the dragonet. In response, Winckelriedt raised his sword in salute and set off in the direction of the creature's abode.

After an arduous climb up the steep slopes of Pilatus, Winckelriedt stood at last inside a long natural corridor, formed by tall, pillarlike rocks, which led to his foe's cave. But even as he began walking toward it, the dragonet charged out and glared at him. It was a surprisingly graceful winged beast, and its size was equally unexpected, for it was scarcely as tall as its human challenger.

Nevertheless, its skill at emitting scorching bolts of fire was more than enough to gain instant respect from Winckelriedt, and a battle ensued that emphasized deft footwork and deflection at the expense of direct combat. But once, as it sought to engulf him in fire, the dragonet's curving neck came too close to Winckelriedt's blade, and one chance was all that he needed to slice through its flesh with a sweep of his sword.

The creature's head fell to the ground and its flashing eyes closed for the last time. Greatly rejoicing, Winckelriedt raised his sword above his head in celebration of his victory. But in so doing, he sealed his fate. A trickle of the dragonet's blood ran down the hilt of the blade onto his hand and wrist. He opened his mouth to scream, but before he could utter a sound he was dead, killed by the avenging blood of the beast that he had slain only moments earlier.

An explanation for the tale of this dragonet may lie in the fact that skeletons of pterodactyls—prehistoric flying reptiles—have been discovered in the locality of Mount Pilatus.

The description of the dragonet, with its slender jaws, long neck, and pointed wings, may have been derived from pterodactyl fossils.

THE LIVING DRAGONS OF
KOMODO AND NEW GUINEA

There is little doubt that many stories featuring classical dragons were inspired by sightings of crocodiles, alligators, and giant lizards.

During innumerable retellings and elaborations of the original accounts, many of these have acquired wings and fire-breathing capabilities. Some of the biggest lizards alive today are the monitors of Africa, Asia, and Australasia, and these would have been particularly effective as models for such monsters. It is no coincidence that their most impressive representative is referred to scientifically as a dragon.

Native to Komodo and three other tiny islands in the Lesser Sundas group of Southeast Asia, the Komodo dragon is the world's largest living lizard, occasionally exceeding 10 feet (3 m) in length. Surprisingly, this colossal creature remained unknown to science until as recently as 1912, but the natives of the region were well aware of its existence and also of its prowess as a man-killer. Heightening its dragonesque appearance is its bright yellow tongue, flickering out of its mouth in faithful facsimile of its mythical, fire-spitting namesakes.

It is not surprising that the Komodo dragon, a ferocious, flesh-eating lizard of monstrous size, should be regarded as a veritable dragon.

There may, however, be an even bigger, more dragonlike form of monitor lizard still awaiting scientific discovery. Tribes in the jungles of Papua New Guinea speak of the *artrellia*, which they claim is a ferocious dragon up to 30 feet (9 m) long, which attacks and kills anyone it encounters. In 1980, "Operation Drake," a scientific expedition led by the explorer John Blashford-Snell, was given a young *artrellia*, which was found to belong to an already known lizard species, called Salvadori's monitor. Adults can reach 15 feet (4.5 m) in length, but are much more slender than the Komodo dragon, and for this reason Salvadori's monitor cannot be classed as the world's largest lizard—unless some weighty 30-foot (9-m) specimen is eventually found.

Chapter

4

Sky Dragons

During their evolution, some serpentine dragons have forfeited terrestrial mastery or aquatic domination in favor of aerial supremacy—spending much of their time drifting, soaring, or actively propelling themselves with wondrous wingbeats, often far above the land and sea, amid the vast cloud-dappled kingdom of the sky.

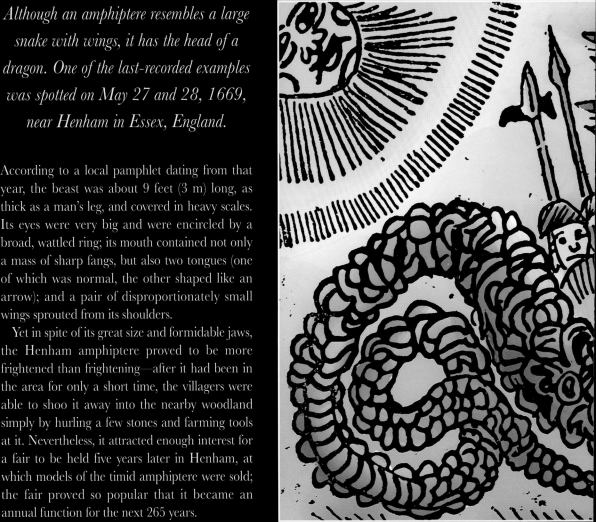

Although an amphiptere resembles a large snake with wings, it has the head of a dragon. One of the last-recorded examples was spotted on May 27 and 28, 1669, near Henham in Essex, England.

According to a local pamphlet dating from that year, the beast was about 9 feet (3 m) long, as thick as a man's leg, and covered in heavy scales. Its eyes were very big and were encircled by a broad, wattled ring; its mouth contained not only a mass of sharp fangs, but also two tongues (one of which was normal, the other shaped like an arrow); and a pair of disproportionately small wings sprouted from its shoulders.

Yet in spite of its great size and formidable jaws, the Henham amphiptere proved to be more frightened than frightening—after it had been in the area for only a short time, the villagers were able to shoo it away into the nearby woodland simply by hurling a few stones and farming tools at it. Nevertheless, it attracted enough interest for a fair to be held five years later in Henham, at which models of the timid amphiptere were sold; the fair proved so popular that it became an annual function for the next 265 years.

The flying dragon of Henham was pictured in a booklet called The Flying Serpent, *first published in 1669. Despite being menaced by farmers with pitchforks and sharpened staves, it looks remarkably cheerful. The villagers capitalized on their dragon (which some said they invented) by instituting an annual fair at which images of it were sold.*

of gum called styrax near the trees because the smoke that it gave off was singularly successful at driving the serpents away.

Long ago, Arabia's winged snakes were so numerous that every spring vast hordes of them would fly toward Egypt, filling the skies with the sound of their beating wings and hissing tongues like a swarm of serpentine locusts. But fortunately for Egypt, they were swiftly vanquished by flocks of ibises—large stork-like birds—which gorged insatiably upon the plague until not a single snake remained alive to enter the country.

For this same reason, Moses' army was equipped with baskets full of living ibises when it attacked the Ethiopians, who had invaded Egypt and penetrated as far as Memphis. By releasing the ibises, Moses made sure that his army's progression was impeded neither by earthbound nor by airborne serpents.

Winged snakes appeared extensively in Egyptian mythology. The evil monster Apep, which nightly battled with the sun god Ra for supremacy, was sometimes depicted as a great serpent with wings. So, too, was Mertseger, goddess of silence and guardian of desert tombs.

Even more frequently portrayed in this guise, however, was the snake goddess Buto, protector of the pharaoh, who assumed the form of a magnificent winged cobra with a crown upon her head. Less commonly, the winged snake was seen as an emblem of Nekhebet, who was a mother goddess and the goddess of childbirth.

Yet if winged snakes were once so abundant and familiar, why are there none alive today? The

reported from many regions of the world. In India, for instance, there was once a particularly lethal, nocturnal variety, whose urine was so toxic that droplets of it would instantly rot the skin of anyone it fell upon as these snakes flew overhead.

Equally memorable were the singing snakes of Sien Mountain in China. Each of these elongated creatures had four wings, their voices sounded like the rattling of stones, and their appearance inevitably presaged a great drought in the neighboring city.

By contrast, Phoenicia's *agathos daimon*—an invisible serpent with a heart-shaped tongue and wings—was deemed to be a benign guardian spirit, hovering unseen around humanity.

The most important region of the world for winged snakes was, it seems, the Middle East. According to the Greek historian Herodotus, writing in the fifth century B.C., immense numbers of these aerial reptiles inhabited Arabia. They occurred in many different colors and were relatively small, but very poisonous, and could be found thronging in the trees that produced the highly prized aromatic gum resin known as frankincense. The frankincense merchants, however, had devised a safe means of obtaining this commodity: they burned a type

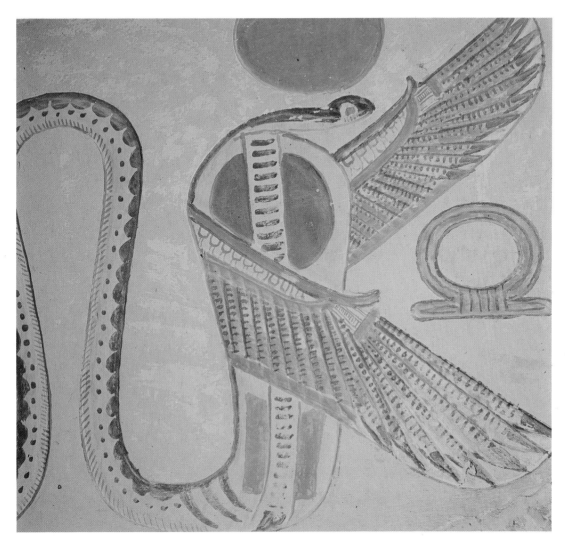

answer may lie in their grotesque mode of reproduction. According to Herodotus, at the precise instant of impregnation between a pair of these creatures, the female would seize the male's neck in a frenzy of passion and continue to bite it until she had completely decapitated her unfortunate mate.

Moreover, instead of laying eggs, the female gave birth to live young—which made their way to the outside world not by any normal birth

An Egyptian tomb painting of a flying serpent from the Valley of the Queens probably represents Mertseger, the snake goddess who guarded the tombs at Thebes.

mechanism, but by the decidedly gruesome means of gnawing through their mother's uterus and then through her intestines, during which process she inevitably perished.

With such a lethal life cycle, it is hardly surprising that winged snakes became extinct!

Quetzalcoatl, Plumed Serpent God of Mexico

It seemed as if the very heavens had burst into a blazing inferno of green fire, and everyone fell to the ground in fear and homage as the sublime vision soared through the sky overhead.

If they had dared to gaze up at its wonder, they would have witnessed the marvel of an immense feathered serpent, every coil garbed in brilliant emerald plumes, streaking like a bolt of molten malachite across the vault of the sky.

When it was far beyond its prone worshippers, the magnificent sky dragon descended to earth, and as the first plumes of its serpentine body brushed against the grass, a spectacular transformation took place. For the briefest moment, the feathered reptile became enveloped by a fiery, incandescent orb of light, which faded to reveal in the serpent's stead a majestic god, robed in glorious raiment fashioned from those same resplendent green plumes and wearing a brilliant turquoise mask shaped like the terrible jaws of a crocodile. It was Quetzalcoatl—feathered snake god of the wind, wisdom, and life.

The history of Quetzalcoatl is one of multiple, transforming identities. As far back as the time of the Maya culture of Mexico's Yucatán peninsula (500 B.C.–A.D. 900), the plumed serpent Kukulcan was an important deity. Similarly, Topiltzin, first king of a fierce warring race called the Toltecs, whose empire in the Valley of Mexico eventually fell during the latter half of the twelfth century,

conferred upon himself the title of Quetzalcoatl. And when the valley was later occupied by an itinerant race that became known as the Aztecs, the feathered serpent Quetzalcoatl was incorporated into their rich pantheon of gods, which was drawn from the legends of the many tribes they had encountered and conquered during their earlier travels.

Quetzalcoatl is identified by zoologists as a mythological fusion of a serpent and a real—but exceptionally spectacular—bird, the quetzal. This bright green species with scarlet underparts, which belongs to the trogon family, is found in Mexico, Guatemala, and as far south as Costa Rica. The male sports four tail feathers of shimmering emerald hue, each more than 2 feet (60 cm) long, which undulate as it flies—conferring upon the bird the exotic appearance of a flying feathered snake.

Central American mythology tells of many fraught encounters between Quetzalcoatl and his implacable enemy, Tezcatlipoca, god of trickery and darkness, whose name refers to the smoky

Aztec kings carried ceremonial shields covered in designs, often of dragons such as this, which were executed entirely in feathers.

Quetzalcoatl is sometimes shown as a man and at other times as a plumed serpent; here he appears in both guises.

mirror of obsidian through which he was able to view the future.

On one occasion, Tezcatlipoca persuaded the young Quetzalcoatl to peer into the depths of this mirror and horrified the youth with visions of how he would be in the distant future—a wizened, enfeebled old man with a pale face and long white beard (curious features not typical of Central American races, yet invariably attributed to Quetzalcoatl).

Another time, Tezcatlipoca succeeded in corrupting the pure-minded serpent god, plying him with wine until he made drunken love to his own sister. Once sober, Quetzalcoatl was so mortified by his debauched actions that he lit a funeral pyre and cast himself upon it—whereupon his ashes were wondrously transformed into a phalanx of gorgeously plumed birds that filled the sky with their dazzling colors, and his glowing heart ascended into the heavens, where it will remain forever as the bright morning star.

But perhaps the most famous, and momentous, of all stories concerning Quetzalcoatl tells of his passing and of his prophesied return. According to Toltec mythology, he was the ruler of Tollan, the principal city of their empire, until Tezcatlipoca decided to destroy the people of Tollan and banish their ruler for all time. Utilizing a series of clever disguises, the evil deity slaughtered great numbers of the Toltecs. After a final disaster, in which he lured all the remaining Toltecs to their doom in a darkened house by the tempting odor of freshly roasted maize, Tezcatlipoca turned his attention to Quetzalcoatl.

In despair at having failed his people, Quetzalcoatl set fire to Tollan and turned away, trekking through the lonely mountains toward the sea. But even as he journeyed upon this last, tragic pilgrimage, his dark nemesis, Tezcatlipoca, pursued the serpent god remorselessly, not content until he had stolen every talent and treasure that he possessed. Consequently, by the time Quetzalcoatl had reached the sea, most of his magical powers had gone, but not all. Gazing out at the rolling waves, he fashioned an extraordinary raft of entwined serpents, upon which he stepped and sailed away to the east.

According to an Aztec prediction, however, the benevolent protector of their race would ultimately return in triumph—and it seemed that this time had arrived, when, one day early in the year 1519, a fleet of ships

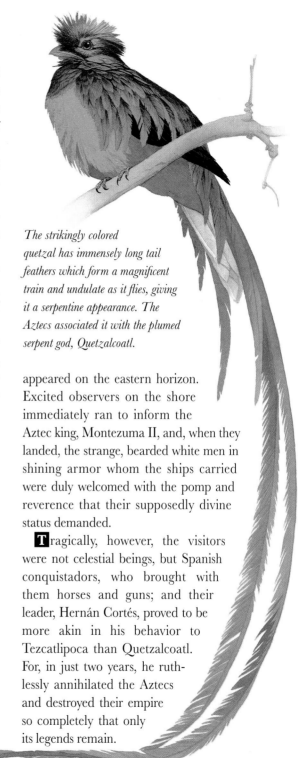

The strikingly colored quetzal has immensely long tail feathers which form a magnificent train and undulate as it flies, giving it a serpentine appearance. The Aztecs associated it with the plumed serpent god, Quetzalcoatl.

appeared on the eastern horizon. Excited observers on the shore immediately ran to inform the Aztec king, Montezuma II, and, when they landed, the strange, bearded white men in shining armor whom the ships carried were duly welcomed with the pomp and reverence that their supposedly divine status demanded.

Tragically, however, the visitors were not celestial beings, but Spanish conquistadors, who brought with them horses and guns; and their leader, Hernán Cortés, proved to be more akin in his behavior to Tezcatlipoca than Quetzalcoatl. For, in just two years, he ruthlessly annihilated the Aztecs and destroyed their empire so completely that only its legends remain.

THE DRAGON
DEITIES OF CHINA

*All the varied types of Oriental
dragon exhibit many fundamental
differences from their Western counterparts.*

Among the most dramatic of these are their ability to fly even when wingless; their shape-shifting capacity, which allows them to adopt innumerable guises (including human forms); their generally benevolent nature and relationship with people; and humanity's own reverence for these ethereal dragons. Indeed, many of the East's most ancient and august human lineages actually claim descent from them.

The most famous category of Oriental dragon is the Chinese dragon, whose serpentine body and ferocious bearded face readily come to mind when considering such creatures. However, its precise morphology, as detailed by the scholar Wang Fu, who was active during the Han dynasty (206 B.C.–A.D. 220), is an extremely complex combination of features drawn from nine very distinct entities.

Thus, the Chinese dragon's head is that of a camel, its eyes are a demon's, its ears a cow's, its horns are the branched antlers of a stag, its neck is a snake's, its belly a clam's. The soles of its feet are a tiger's, while its claws are an eagle's, and the 117 scales sheathing its long body are those of a carp. Of these scales, 81 are infused with benevolent essence (*yang*) and 36 with malign essence (*yin*)—for although Oriental dragons are primarily benign, their influence can sometimes be

malevolent, too. Even its voice is ambivalent: likened to the jingling of copper pans, it is neither mellifluous nor cacophonous.

As for its dexterity in becoming airborne without wings, this talent stems from the *chi'ih muh*, a bladder-like swelling on top of its head; and the male dragon's potent power is derived from a large, luminous pearl concealed under its chin or throat by folds of skin.

Unlike its Western relatives, the Chinese dragon undergoes a series of profound metamorphic transformations during its gradual progress from hatchling to mature dragon—a lengthy process spanning 3,000 years. Hatched from a brightly colored gemlike egg laid a millennium earlier, its first physical phase is that of a water snake (Chinese dragons

*Dragons often adorned the clothes
of important officials; this four-
toed golden dragon with silver
claws was embroidered in silk
and gold on a mandarin's robe.*

are always closely associated with water, particularly rain), which takes 500 years to develop the head of a carp. It is now known as a *kiao*. Transformation of a fishlike nature continues for a further millennium, by which time it has also acquired a carp's scales. In general appearance, however, it has become an anguinine dragon, with four short limbs, an elongated tail and face, a profuse beard, and four sharp claws on each foot.

At this stage in its physical advancement, the dragon is called a *kiao-lung* or simply a *lung*, which translates as "deaf"; for although it has ears, they are not functional. During the next 500 years, however, the *lung* grows a pair of horns—through which it can hear.

By then, it is known as a *kioh-lung*, and this is the most familiar form of Chinese dragon; but its metamorphosis is still not complete. Yet another millennium is required in order for it to gain the rarest characteristics of the Oriental dragon, a series of branching wings. Fully mature at last, the winged dragon is termed a *ying-lung* and is truly a wonder to behold.

There are numerous types of Chinese dragon, but four of these are especially important. The *t'ien lung* is the celestial dragon, protector of the

Ceramic wall tiles in the Cultural Centre in Hong Kong depict a dragon playing with the pearl, representing power and wisdom, that the male dragon keeps beneath its chin.

heavens and guardian of the gods' heavenly abodes. Of equal significance is the *shen-lung*, or spiritual dragon, the azure-scaled master of storms and skyborne bringer of rain.

The splendid robes and regalia of Chinese emperors were richly adorned with a special rank of *shen-lung*: the five-toed imperial dragon, which only the emperor was permitted to use for decorative purposes. The penalty imposed upon anyone appropriating this insignia was death.

The *ti-lung* is the dragon of land, stream, and river, which spends springtime in heaven and autumn in the sea. And the *fu-ts'ang lung* is the treasure dragon—keeper of secret hoards of priceless jewels and precious metals within the deepest, darkest vaults of the earth.

Other notable dragons include the yellow dragon or dragon horse, a divine messenger that arose from the River Lo, revealing the eight trigrams of the system of divination known as I Ching; the human-bodied fire dragon, or *lung wang*—the immortal dragon king, inhabiting an opulent palace on the ocean floor; and the

The ocean-dwelling lung wang, *or dragon king, illustrated in* The Dragon, Image and Demon *by Hampden C. du Bose.*

thunder dragon, with obsidian scales, which often transforms itself into a small boy whose skin is bright ultramarine and who rides upon a scarlet carp.

Perhaps the oddest Chinese dragon is the *t'ao t'ieh*. Although it has only one head and a single pair of forelegs, it has two bodies, each with its own pair of hind legs and its own tail. Exiled to the outer darkness of space in the second millennium B.C. by the emperor Shin, this six-legged monster personifies gluttony, which is the literal translation of its name, and it is often depicted on dishes as a deterrent to greed.

Creating a striking image of symmetry, with a central head and a body on each side, the *t'ao t'ieh* is a popular choice for artists seeking a symmetrical subject to occupy the center of a frieze or the corner of an ornamental carving, and it frequently appears on early Chinese sacrificial bronzes.

There is even a fish-shaped dragon called the *yu lung*, which symbolizes success in passing examinations. Evidently, there is a dragon for every contingency in Chinese life.

Songbirds of Sadness, Dragons of Despair

*The dragons of Japan are superficially
similar to those of China, but are more serpentine
in shape, sport only three claws on each foot,
and are less predominantly aerial.*

The most familiar type is the *tatsu*, which is descended from a primitive three-toed variety of Chinese dragon. Unlike its ancestor, it is traditionally associated more intimately with the sea than with rain—for Japan is less vulnerable than China to drought-related devastation, reducing the necessity to pray to rain-releasing dragon deities.

Far more grotesque was the eight-headed dragon confronted by Susa-no-wo, brother of Japan's fair sun goddess, Ama-terasu. While traveling beside the River Hi-no-ka-mi in the province of Izumo, Susa-no-wo encountered a beautiful young maiden in the company of an elderly couple, all three of them greatly distraught. Asking why they were weeping, he learned that the man and woman were the parents of the maiden, who was the last of their eight daughters, and that every year for the past seven, one of their daughters had been abducted and devoured by a dragon from Koshi. Soon it would return for the final time, for their last beloved daughter, Kush-inada-hime.

The dragon was a terrible beast, so enormous that its mighty body spanned eight hills and eight valleys, and with trees and moss sprouting upon its scabrous hide. It possessed eight thrashing tails, eight hideous heads, each with eyes as red as the Japanese winter cherry, and had a repulsively inflamed belly. No mortal could vanquish such a monster, but Susa-no-wo was more than mortal. In return for Kush-inada-hime's hand in marriage, he pledged to destroy their reptilian enemy, and when her joyful parents freely gave their consent, Susa-no-wo set to work at once to engineer the dragon's swift demise.

After transforming his bride-to-be into an innocuous comb, which he hid in his hair, Susa-no-wo instructed her parents to brew a great quantity of potent sake, and as soon as it was prepared, to pour it into eight colossal vats. A tall palisade was then constructed, pierced by eight gates; behind each of the gates was a long bench, and placed upon each bench was a vat of sake. As soon as this was set up, Susa-no-wo and Kush-inada-hime's parents concealed themselves nearby to await the dragon's arrival.

As anticipated, the sake's rich bouquet was an effective bait, enticing the monster to visit the

*This print by Kunisada probably depicts the
legendary female sage Tai-shin flying across
the ocean on the back of a white dragon.*

compound and sample the liquid lure behind the gates. With gluttonous glee, each of its eight heads swiftly quaffed a vat of sake, and inevitably, the dragon soon became exceedingly inebriated—so much so that it sank to the ground in a drunken stupor.

Losing no time, Susa-no-wo emerged from his hiding place, raised his powerful two-handed sword skyward, and hacked the comatose beast into a myriad fragments, until the Hi-no-ka-mi was transformed into a river of crimson blood.

So ended the dragon of Koshi, and so began Susa-no-wo's settlement in Izumo with his new wife—and a new sword, too. For inside one of the slain monster's tails, he had discovered to his appreciable surprise a wonderful, keen-edged blade, the *kusa-nagi-no-tachi*, or herb-quelling dragon sword, which he subsequently gave to his sun goddess sister.

Very different from the Koshi dragon, but no less exotic in appearance, is the *hai riyo*—also known as the *tobi tatsu*, *schachi hoko*, or dragon bird. There are several depictions of this remarkable creature on the ornamental screens decorating the Chi-on-in monastery in Kyoto, and although it supposedly comprises the Japanese equivalent of China's winged dragon, or *ying-lung*, it bears little physical similarity.

Eschewing the sinuous, scaly body of the *ying-lung*, the *hai riyo* is portrayed with the feathered wings, body, and tail of a bird, and with its clawed feet; but it retains the unmistakable, beard-fringed visage of a dragon. Moreover, transformations of dragons into birds occur quite frequently in

A ferocious-looking creature, the hai riyo, *or dragon bird, is the Japanese equivalent of the Chinese* ying-lung, *the most advanced form of dragon.*

Japan. The scene of one reputedly regular instance is an extremely large pond called Ukisima, situated in the eastern part of Fu-si-mi-shi-ro-yama, at Yama-shiro, near Kyoto. During the warm summer months, children often play around its perimeter or wade near its shore, but no one ever swims toward the center, for that is the deep-water domain of a great white dragon with sleek opalescent scales.

This beast is a source of dread and despair to the local populace, for every 50 years it assumes the form of an *o-gon-cho*, a golden-plumed songbird, but its song brings sadness, not joy, and resembles the bloodcurdling howl of a wolf. The sight of this feathered nemesis, or the sound of its eerie voice, inevitably presages a season of terrible famine and pestilence, during which many people will die. The *o-gon-cho* was believed to have been seen as recently as April 1834, and widespread starvation and an outbreak of disease did indeed occur in the area shortly afterward. Its feathers may be gilded and bright, but its eldritch voice will always betray the true nature of this dragon-derived bird of ill omen.

Despite their exalted, often divine, status, Japanese dragons are not without enemies. Among the most troublesome of these are the fox spirits, which carry unclean objects to ensure that dragons will not attack them in retaliation for their trickery. Fox spirits also enjoy tormenting people and often assume a human guise for this purpose. They live for 1,000 years and become masters of illusion as they mature; but should a relatively young individual disguise itself as a human, it can easily be identified, for if it stands by a pool, it will be betrayed by its reflection in the water, which will be that of a fox.

As their name suggests, fox spirits frequently appear as foxes, too—but in this disguise they can be recognized by the yellow tongues of flickering flame that momentarily materialize above their heads. Only when they have lived on earth for 1,000 years do they turn aside from villainy, whereupon their silky pelage turns white or golden, they sprout nine magnificent tails and then ascend to heaven. Still magically adept, but no longer wicked, the fox spirits

Animals modeled by Japanese potters always seem to have a humorous aspect; this cheerful-looking Kakiemon dragon is no exception.

are now sinless beings who control and assist agricultural activity on earth.

In an article in the journal *Scientific American*, dating from 1916, J. O'Malley Irwin suggested that the longstanding, traditional Eastern belief in Japanese and Chinese dragons may have arisen from early findings in Asia of fossils of giant sauropod dinosaurs (*see p.72*). Indeed, some spectacular skeletons of a huge Oriental species of sauropod related to the American *Morosaurus* (also known as *Camarasaurus*) were discovered by Irwin and his wife during November 1915 while they were exploring a large cave called Shen K'an Tzu, on the right bank of the Yangtze River near to the Ichang Gorge.

The acclaimed American scientist Dr. Carl Sagan has taken the subject of dinosaur-associated dragon origins even farther. In his book *The Dragons of Eden* (1977), he boldly proposed that dragon-based myths and legends may stem from racial memories of dinosaurs passed down to us from the earliest mammals, small, shrew-like creatures living during prehistoric times that scuttled along timidly in the shadow of these reptilian giants. There is no doubt that dragons and certain dinosaurs (especially some of the larger predatory types) do exhibit a surprising outward similarity. Is this just coincidence, or the distorted reflection of a far-distant recollection? Who can say?

THE WINGED
SERPENTS OF WALES

As recently as the mid-1800s, flying snakes of amazing beauty, with ornate feathered wings, were believed to inhabit Glamorgan in Wales.

According to one old man who lived at Penllyne in Glamorgan and died early in the twentieth century, the woods around Penllyne Castle contained many of these extraordinary creatures when he was a boy. They were said to be brilliant in color, as if spangled with sparkling gemstones, and, like the peacock's train, their wings often bore eyes; some also had rainbow-hued crests.

Yet despite their exquisite appearance, the winged serpents were slaughtered by local people as if they were merely vermin because they preyed upon the farmers' poultry. Indeed, the old man's father and uncle had killed several when he was a youngster. Now, they were apparently extinct. Flying serpents were also reported at Penmark Place, where one elderly woman claimed that there had even been a "king" and "queen" of these winged wonders.

If such serpents really did exist, what could they have been? Millions of years ago, Britain was home to *Kuehneosaurus*, an elongated lizardlike beast, whose ribs were extended to form a pair of membranous winglike structures that may have enabled it to glide through the air. Today, a similar creature still exists in the humid jungles of Southeast Asia and is aptly known as *Draco volans*, or "flying dragon." It is not native to Europe, however, and even if some had escaped from captivity into the woodlands of Wales, they would not have survived in its climate.

It has been suggested that brightly colored serpents with feathered wings spied in the Vale of Edeyrnion in 1812 may have been cock pheasants, which were unfamiliar there. But this theory does not explain the serpents' liking for poultry, and it is not likely that a pheasant could be mistaken for a flying snake.

There might once have been proof of their existence, for the Penmark woman stated that her grandfather had killed one of these beasts and kept its feathered skin until, after he died, his relatives discarded it. If they had been less eager to do so, science may have been able to unveil the identity of Wales's winged serpents.

One of the earliest lizards, Kuehneosaurus *had membranous flaps that enabled it to glide.*

NEO-DRAGONS

*The heterogeneous assemblage of monsters
known as neo-dragons may not be true dragons
in the strictest zoo-mythological sense, but as
their tempestuous confrontations with humans
down the ages have demonstrated, such
pretenders as the basilisk, hydra, peluda,
and other imitators are as dramatically
dragonesque in behavior and appearance
as any of their bona-fide brethren.*

From Basilisk to Cockatrice

In early times, one of the most feared monsters in the Western world was the basilisk, a small but horrific reptile, hailed as king of the serpents.

Disdaining the craven, belly-crawling mode of locomotion adopted by its accursed subjects, the basilisk held the upper part of its 2-foot (60-cm) long, saffron-scaled body proudly erect as it glided across the ground. Upon its head it bore a crown of sorts, composed of three white tubercles that resembled a silver diadem. Its regal status was also acknowledged in its names—*basilisk* is Greek for "little king," which is the translation of its Latin name, *regulus*, too.

Despite its diminutive size, the basilisk was a near-implacable foe to all that it encountered. It could kill the largest animal and split asunder the biggest boulder with a single glance from its deadly eyes. Its noxious breath withered the sturdiest tree or bush and permanently poisoned any stream or river from which it drank; even the foul odor of its sweat was toxic. It could cause birds flying overhead to drop lifeless to the ground, simply by spitting its envenomed saliva up into the air. And any fertile land through which this abhorrent beast traveled became an arid, lifeless desert.

Only three living things could counter the basilisk's lethal powers—the weasel, which was somehow immune to its death-dealing gaze; the rooster, whose raucous crowing would send the serpent king fleeing in fright; and rue, a plant that could withstand the basilisk's breath, and which was used by weasels to heal themselves if they were injured during battles with this monster.

In medieval times, however, the basilisk underwent a dramatic metamorphosis (at least in the documents of its chroniclers). It acquired birdlike legs (usually two, but occasionally as many as eight), as well as a coiling tail and, eventually, a pair of wings, so evolving into a beast reminiscent of a wyvern, but with certain clearly defined differences. For although its body and tail retained their reptilian scales, its wings became feathered, and its head transformed into that of its erstwhile vanquisher—the rooster. Wattles hung down from either side of its face, its jaws became a horny beak, and it even acquired its enemy's ability to crow.

Ultimately, its name changed too. No longer the basilisk, king of serpents, this counterfeit cockerel now became known by a name that emphasized its fowl-impersonating features instead—the cockatrice. But most bizarre of all

The cockatrice, which evolved from the basilisk, was an impressive creature with features of both dragon and rooster.

was the means by which such a horrendous composite of rooster and reptile was created. Whereas it had been assumed that basilisks simply hatched from eggs laid by others of their kind (the mode of reproduction practiced by many species of snake), the cockatrice's origin was much more exotic. It was hatched in dung by a toad from a round, leathery, shell-less egg that had been laid by a seven-year-old rooster when the dog star, Sirius, was in the ascendant.

As far as its behavior was concerned, however, the cockatrice was just as gruesome as its serpentine ancestor. But fortunately, there was at least one successful method known for destroying this pestilential creature, and this was efficaciously employed during the Middle Ages against the ferocious cockatrice of Wherwell, a village in Hampshire, England.

After hatching from an egg incubated by a toad in the cellar of Wherwell Priory, this fiendish creature had been innocently reared as a pet by

The cockatrice reported from Lake Fagua in Chile was a huge and most unusual beast, with two tails and the face of a man; it was later discovered to be a hoax.

A drawing based on descriptions of the African crowing crested cobra shows how the attributes of a rooster are allied to its snakelike body and fangs.

the priory's nuns until its true nature had become apparent. Thereafter, it had secreted itself in the cellar, emerging periodically to devour local livestock and assault, or even slay, anyone who confronted it.

Its tyrannous reign was ended when a priory servant utilized his knowledge of ancient lore to destroy this terrible monster. The gaze of a cockatrice is so searing that it is fatal even to other cockatrices, and so the man cunningly lowered a steel mirror down into the cellar where the creature dwelt. Seeing its reflection, the cockatrice instantly attacked, believing it to be an intruder, but the sight of its own hideous image was so shocking that the monster promptly perished.

The basilisk and cockatrice were largely confined to northern Africa and western Europe, but similar creatures have been reported in many other parts of the world. Iceland's equivalent was a basilisklike beast called the skoffin, which could only be killed by the gaze of another skoffin, or by shooting it with a silver button upon which had been carved the sign of the Cross. In 1784, a man-faced cockatrice with donkey's ears, the horns of a bull, and two tails (one for gripping its prey, the other for killing it) was reported in Lake Fagua in Chile, from where it emerged at night to devour oxen and pigs. Not too surprisingly, it subsequently proved to be an elaborate hoax.

By contrast, while in Jamaica in 1845–46, the English naturalist Philip Gosse collected many serious eyewitness accounts of a mysterious wattled snake that could allegedly crow like a rooster—a true basilisk exhibiting the first stages of metamorphosis into a cockatrice? And a much larger, highly venomous counterpart, called the *inkhomi* (killer), or crowing crested cobra, has for centuries been reliably reported in Central Africa by locals and Western travelers alike. Partial remains of this controversial serpent have occasionally been obtained, but never formally identified with any species known to science.

As with the still uncaptured tatzelworm, which may be the elusive real-life inspiration for the lindorm, could it be that the basilisk and cockatrice are more than a myth? Perhaps there are living versions still awaiting scientific discovery in Africa and the West Indies. It would not be the first time that a creature of legend has proved to be one of reality, too.

In this medieval representation, the basilisk still has its crown and serpentine shape, but has acquired the legs, beak, and wattles of a cockatrice.

Terror of the Tarasque

France in the Middle Ages was a land of lingering, legendary monsters— anachronistic abominations left over from primeval ages.

Singularly horrific was a neo-dragon called the tarasque. It was spawned by the biblical monster Leviathan and originally lived in Galatia, in Asia Minor, but had come to haunt the banks of the River Rhône between Avignon and Arles in southern France.

One evening, as the shadow of night was falling, a traveler named Jacques du Bois quickened his step as he journeyed along the bank of the river. Nervously, he scanned its sable waters and the forbidding gloom of the fringing forest—his eyes questing for something that he fervently prayed he would not have the misfortune to see.

Du Bois had heard terrifying rumors that a hideous creature called the tarasque had taken up residence along this stretch of the river. Here it held in thrall the hapless populace of nearby Nerluc, a once tranquil country town whose inhabitants and livestock were now the focus of its relentless depredations. But it also devoured any unfortunate wayfarer passing that way who was unwary enough not to perceive the proximity of this rapacious monster.

Distracted by such grisly thoughts flowing unchecked through his mind, the traveler fatally

An ornamental metal plaque, now in the Musée des Arts et Traditions Populaires in Paris, shows the tarasque devouring a man.

ignored a deep, thunderous rumble emanating from a shadowy glade just ahead. Suddenly, the forest seemed to erupt, disgorging from its hidden depths a macabre vision spawned by the darkest and most bizarre of nightmares.

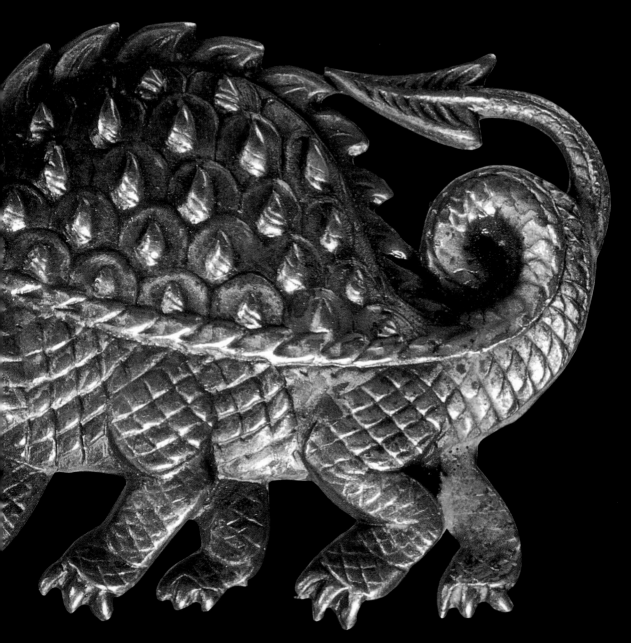

Larger in size than the biggest horse or burliest ox, the tarasque stood on six powerful limbs equipped with the murderous paws of a giant bear, and furiously switched its long viperine tail from side to side like living whipcord. The magnificent mane of its leonine head flowed like a burnished golden sea around its shoulders, and its teeth were great ivory daggers of death. Most extraordinary of all, however, was the massive carapace encrusting its back. Resembling the shell of a colossal tortoise, it bristled with an armory of mighty spikes, rendering the monster invincible to any form of attack.

It was for good reason, therefore, that the ill-fated Jacques du Bois knew his life to be at an end—an end so swift that he did not even have time to scream. As he gazed motionless at his destroyer, like a songbird mesmerized by the hypnotic stare of a serpent, the tarasque opened its fearsome jaws and let out a deafening roar, accompanied by a stream of fire that curled around its luckless victim and ignited his flesh like tinder.

As time went by, the people of Nerluc grew more and more desperate to be free from the tarasque's unremitting tyranny. On one occasion, 16 of the town's bravest men marched out to do battle with their adversary—but to no avail. In a matter of moments, half of their number had been incinerated by a single blast of flame belched from the monster's gullet, and the remaining eight fled back to the town, fortunate to have survived their ordeal.

Nerluc seemed doomed and destined for destruction; but then someone came along who may well have seemed, at least to an outsider, to be the most unlikely vanquisher of dragons. One day, a small boat docked at Saintes-Maries-de-la-Mer,

A carving of St. Martha, with the docile tarasque at her feet, appears on a stone altarpiece, dating from 1470, in the Cathedral of Saint-Sauveur in Aix-en-Provence.

and out of it stepped a young, lissom maiden, fresh faced and wearing a simple dress of pure white. Her fame had spread far and wide, for this unassuming figure, with her gentle demeanor, was St. Martha, whose inspirational preaching and acts of selfless beneficence had brought joy and hope to all who met her.

As soon as her arrival became known, the townspeople of Nerluc flocked to meet her and tearfully implored her to free them from the terrible oppression of the tarasque. St. Martha promised to do everything she could to help them and, without further ado, she walked through the outlying fields toward the forest bordering the river that harbored her terrifying quarry.

She did not have to search for long. Within only a few minutes of entering the woodland, she spied the tarasque in a sunlit clearing, where it was devouring the remains of its latest victim, a local herdsman.

So intent was the monster upon its gory repast that it remained totally unaware of her presence, enabling the saint to approach to within an arm's length of its gleaming carapace and rippling mane and also to pick up two branches that had recently been charred by its fiery breath. At that moment, however, the tarasque sensed her presence and whirled around, its eyes blazing.

Edit. Cournand

TARASCON — Procession de la Tarasque

A picture of the festival at Whitsun in 1905 shows a model of the dragon, carried by the men of Tarascon and led by a young girl symbolizing St. Martha.

Instantly, Martha raised the two branches and held them before her monstrous adversary in the shape of the Cross.

As she did so, the tarasque's eyes dimmed, their incandescence replaced by a mellow golden hue, and the mighty creature lay passively at the saint's feet, overcome by bemusement and unwonted peace. Martha bent down and sprinkled holy water all over the subdued dragon. Then she wove a huge collar with braids of her hair and led the tarasque amiably back to Nerluc.

This astonishing spectacle—the bloodthirsty tarasque, tethered and docile as a tame puppy— initially rendered the townspeople speechless and immobile. Once their fear of their longstanding enemy had subsided, however, they grew bolder, coming up to the beast and touching it, then hitting, punching, and kicking it, and hurling rocks and sticks at it, as their anger at its former atrocities burst forth in an uncontrollable tide of hatred and revenge.

The tarasque cowered in fright at this sustained onslaught, and St. Martha pleaded with the horde to forgive the beast and let it live in its new, transformed state; but it was too late. Whether due to direct physical attack or to the almost tangible weight of loathing heaped upon it, the tarasque suddenly rolled over and died.

Memory of this monster is manifest even today. As a lasting reminder of its former tribulations, Nerluc is now called Tarascon, and it stages a tarasque festival each Whitsun, while the town's official seal depicts the former oppressor in all its terrible splendor.

THE PELUDA

On the bank of the River Huisne, at La Ferté-Bernard in medieval France, something was definitely moving.

Suddenly, what appeared at first to be the head and sinuous body of a huge viperlike snake emerged from a spherical mass of bright green vegetation and reared upward above it. Moments later, however, the vegetation itself began to move, quivering as if it were a living creature—for that is precisely what it was. What had seemed to be nothing more than a clump of riverside foliage was in reality the round body of a huge animal with shaggy green fur, and what had appeared to be a giant serpent was now exposed as this extraordinary animal's head and neck.

It was the peluda—a terrifying amphibious neo-dragon, also known as the shaggy beast, which had been spawned in early biblical times and refused entry to Noah's Ark, yet had nonetheless survived the Great Flood and was now terrorizing the environs of La Ferté-Bernard. Its dense green pelage partially hid four horny, turtlelike feet and bristled with countless numbers of spiny quills. These contained potent stinging venom and could be jettisoned like poisonous javelins into anything unwary enough to approach too close. This monstrous beast could also kill a person with a mighty thwack of its powerful tail, and when it was sufficiently angered, a single blast of flame spewed from its throat could incinerate fields for miles around.

For a time, the peluda had contented itself with raiding farms and stables each night in search of livestock as prey—robbing the farmers of their livelihood, but rarely of their lives, unless they were foolish enough to challenge it.

Occasionally, massed attacks on the beast by brave companies drawn from the local populace had succeeded in driving it into the Huisne. But the peluda was of such colossal size that whenever it submerged itself, the river overflowed its banks, and much of the district on both sides was flooded, affecting the farmers' wellbeing just as disastrously as the monster's own onslaughts.

More recently, however, the peluda had added children and damsels to its menu. Several of the fairest maidens had already been devoured, and on that fateful morning it was carrying away yet another—but she was not alone. Her valiant fiancé witnessed the terrible deed and, swearing vengeance, he took up his sword to do battle.

Protected from the peluda's deadly arsenal of quills by his suit of mail, and armed also with knowledge gained from the village's wisest seer, the bold youth strode forth. He aimed a terrible blow with his sword, but not at the monster's undulating neck, nor even at the heaving belly concealed beneath its shaggy fur. Instead, he

The peluda was covered in green fur and had poisonous quills, reminiscent of those of a porcupine, which it could fire at its foes.

hacked at its writhing tail and severed it with a single slash of his keen blade. Instantly, the mighty peluda keeled over and died, for its tail was the only part of its body vulnerable to mortal injury. Back in La Ferté-Bernard, there was great rejoicing, and the remains of the peluda were embalmed. Its conqueror was acclaimed as a hero, and rightly so—after all, he had achieved something that not even the Great Flood had been able to accomplish.

HERCULES AND THE
LERNAEAN HYDRA

*The union of Typhon, a terrifying
hundred-headed giant, and his bride, the
serpent-bodied Echidna, spawned some
of the most gruesome monsters in ancient Greece.*

Among them were the Chimera, a lion-headed monstrosity with a goat's head sprouting from its back and a living serpent for a tail; and the dragon Ladon, ferocious protector of the garden of the Hesperides and its golden apples. There were also Orthos, a fearful hound with two heads; and his even more hideous brother, the three-headed hell-hound Cerberus. But none was more horrifying than the hydra, the most dreadful member of this vile brood.

Little wonder then that even the fearless hero Hercules was somewhat apprehensive as he stood outside the vast, dank cave at Lerna that harbored this monstrous creature. As the second of his 12 great labors, he had been sent to this tormented district of Argolis, in southern Greece, by King Eurystheus, who had commanded him to liberate Lerna by slaying the hydra. This loathsome creature

was willfully slaughtering the district's populace and blighting its countryside, transforming it into a gloomy wilderness of marshland.

Assisted by his nephew Iolaus, who had faithfully accompanied him on this dangerous mission, Hercules lit a series of torches, which they had fashioned from bundles of grass, and fired them into the hydra's grim lair in order to expel its foul occupant. Great clouds of evil-smelling smoke billowed out of the cave mouth, and at the very heart of this choking mass of fumes, something writhed and roared.

The two men backed away, coughing and wiping their streaming eyes; and when they looked back, they beheld a sight so dreadful that even Hercules' fiery blood ran cold in his veins. The acrid smoke had dispelled, exposing a vast bloated mass of pulsating flesh, obscenely corpulent and of a sickeningly pallid hue.

*An unusual corsage ornament
in gold and enamel inspired by
the nine-headed hydra.*

*This romanticized 19th-century
painting shows Hercules slaying
an unexpectedly cobralike hydra.*

In Bernard Picat's engraving, Hercules appears as a typically robust Greek hero, with a serpentine hydra whose heads replicate themselves as rapidly as he clubs them.

Superficially, it resembled a grotesque octopus or squid, for above this obese sac of a body thrashed a flailing mass of tentaclelike appendages—but that was where any such similarity abruptly ended. For as Hercules and Iolaus could see only too clearly, these "tentacles" were, in fact, nine powerful necks, and each of the necks terminated in an evil, horned head, the head of a dragon. This, then, was Hercules' grisly adversary—the Lernaean hydra. When its heads spied Hercules, they emitted a deafening sibilation of hissing fury that whistled through his ears like a thousand shrieking ghosts, and each lunged forward, intent upon seizing this puny, vainglorious human in its bone-crunching jaws.

Undaunted, Hercules raised his mighty club and swung it down with terrible force, crushing into a shapeless mass the skull of the nearest of the nine heads; but, to his horror, the head did not die. Instead, its flattened cranium promptly expanded, enlarged, and split into two, and each of the two halves immediately transformed into a head. From the single original version, shattered by Hercules' club, two brand-new heads had instantly regenerated! Moreover, this deadly duplication occurred every time that he succeeded in destroying one of the creature's many heads.

Soon, the hydra would possess such a quantity of heads that it would certainly quash even the most exalted Greek hero's unrivaled prowess at annihilating monsters, unless he could devise a method of preventing them from replicating themselves. Glancing at the smoldering sheaves of grass that he had used to drive the beast from its cavernous retreat, Hercules suddenly saw an answer to his dilemma, and he quickly set Iolaus to work, preparing a new set of flaming torches.

Yet another of the hydra's heads swung down, jaws fully agape in a bid to grasp Hercules with its

A tapestry in the castle at Angers, France, shows St. John witnessing the seven-headed dragon of the Apocalypse handing over its staff to the leopard-headed beast from the sea, to whom the dragon, once earth-bound, delegated its power.

venomous fangs, and once again he crushed its skull with a single crunching blow of his bloodied club. But before it could begin to divide into two new heads, Iolaus handed him a fiery brand, which he thrust into the gory pulp of the original smashed skull. The flames incinerated its flesh, which meant that it could no longer replicate itself—Hercules had discovered the secret of destroying the hydra.

From that moment on, the battle became increasingly one-sided. Each head that attacked was swiftly destroyed with physical force and burning flame until, at last, only a single head remained. Uniquely, this one was immune to the scorching blast of fire, but not to the single merciless, decapitating thrust that it received from Hercules' razor-sharp sword.

The most terrible neo-dragon that the world had ever seen was no more, and never would be again—not even Typhon and Echidna could spawn its like a second time.

Another famous many-headed neo-dragon was the winged, seven-headed dragon of the Apocalypse, which was scarlet in color and bore ten horns and seven crowns. This was the guise assumed by the devil, who fought with his rebel angels against the valiant St. Michael and the mighty host of Heaven, as narrated in the Revelation of St. John the Divine. Ultimately, St. Michael cast out the dragon, hurling him down to earth with his mutinous acolytes.

THE SALAMANDER
AND THE PYRALLIS

*One evening in 1505, when the Renaissance
sculptor Benvenuto Cellini was five years old, he
was sitting by a great log fire with his father, who
suddenly spotted a small lizardlike beast at
the very heart of the blaze.*

The creature was disporting itself merrily, wreathed in flames, yet ostensibly unharmed by their searing caresses. Greatly excited, Cellini's father pointed it out to his son—and to make sure that the boy never forgot this amazing spectacle, he soundly boxed his ears. A somewhat drastic memory aid, no doubt, but he had good reason for his enthusiastic fervor—he believed the beast frolicking in the fire to be a salamander, one of the most astonishing of all neo-dragons.

Resembling a somewhat doglike lizard, the salamander featured in accounts dating back as far as the ancient Greek philosopher Aristotle and the Roman historian Pliny the Elder. According to these and other early writers, this extraordinary animal was so cold that, simply by stepping into a fire, it could immediately extinguish the flames, assisted by a strange milky fluid that exuded from the many star-shaped markings richly decorating its bright golden skin, and which it could also spit like vitriolic foam from its mouth.

This fluid was lethal not only to fire, but also to life—the skin of anyone touched by it would shrivel and the hair would fall out, creating a hideous, leprous appearance. Furthermore, if a salamander were to fall into a pond or well, the water would be irrevocably envenomed. Drinking from a stream poisoned in this way was blamed for the deaths in India of 2,000 horses and 4,000 soldiers under the command of Alexander the Great.

The bite from a salamander was fatal, too, but one animal could prey upon this toxic beast without suffering any ill effects—the pig. Even so, anyone eating the flesh of a pig that had devoured a salamander would swiftly die—implying that whereas the pig itself was immune to this poison, it retained the creature's deadly fluid within its own tissues.

Symbol of indestructibility, the salamander was depicted in the center of the flames c.1600 by Michael Maior in his book **Atalante Suyant.**

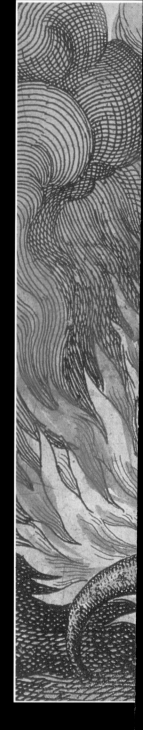

Like the basilisk, during the Middle Ages, the salamander underwent a profound evolutionary transformation. From a beast that could douse flames by virtue of its own icy nature, it became a creature that actively thrived amid blazing fires, furnaces, and even volcanic lava—neither destroying nor being destroyed by their scorching heat. The dramatic power of such a concept appealed to the imagination of King Francis I of France, who adopted the image of a salamander bathed in flames as his personal emblem.

The salamander was of great interest to medieval alchemists because of its reputed ability not only to resist the flames, but actually to thrive within the fire.

This metamorphosed monster was also credited with the ability to spin cocoons of a furry, fireproof substance termed salamander's wool, which, in reality, was asbestos. Many notable personages reputedly possessed artifacts or garments woven from this wonderful material; even Pope Alexander III was said to own a fireproof tunic.

One of the most mysterious personages of medieval times was Prester John, said to be an indescribably wealthy priest-king who ruled over a Christian land of endless wonders somewhere in the East. According to legend, his realm extended beyond India and stretched west toward Babylon. During the twelfth century, the Byzantine emperor Manuel Comnenus received a lengthy letter purportedly written by Prester John, in which he referred to many of his land's animals; among these was the salamander.

Presumably, however, it had metamorphosed yet again, for this salamander seems to have been an exotic form of worm: "In one of our lands, hight Zone, are worms called in our tongue salamanders. These worms can only live in fire, and they build cocoons like silkworms, which are unwound by the ladies of our palace and spun into cloth and dresses, which are worn by our Exaltedness. These dresses, when we would wash and clean them, are cast into flames."

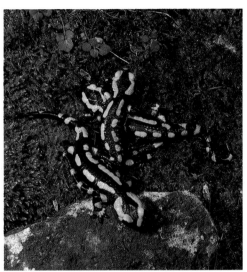

Fire salamanders, 7–9½ inches (18–24 cm) long, are named after their mythical counterpart and are native to hilly regions of central and southern Europe.

Some scholars believe that this ruler's fabulous kingdom may have been real, proposing Ethiopia as its likeliest identity—a country that has been Christian since the fourth century A.D. Similarly, it has been suggested that "John" is a corruption of "Zan," the royal title in Ethiopia. Even so, his letter is nowadays generally dismissed as a hoax, and Prester John's land has long since vanished from the world's atlases.

Today, the incombustible salamander is long gone, too—replaced in zoological tomes by its real-life, newtlike namesakes, which prefer damp holes and logs to sizzling flames, although they do secrete a poisonous white fluid from their skin like their legendary predecessor. And perhaps, in ages past, if a log thrown on a fire had happened to contain one of these living salamanders, its sudden, unexpected emergence in the depths of the blaze may have inspired tales of a wonderful, fire-dwelling beast, which could explain Cellini's sighting. Of such chance occurrences are legends born.

A completely different neo-dragon, but one even more at home in the middle of a blazing fire than the salamander, was a tiny beast termed the pyrallis, pyragones, or pyrausta. This remarkable animal, no bigger than a large fly, resembled a four-legged insect, with a burnished bronze body and golden filigree wings—but its head was that of a dragon.

It was associated exclusively with the copper smelting forges and foundries of Cyprus, in which swarms of the creatures were reported to dance and cavort like incandescent will-o'-the-wisps. Yet if one of these animate sparks should fly out of the flames, even for the briefest of instants, it would die at once—because the pyrallis drew not merely its sustenance, but also its very life force from the furnace's burning heat and raging vitality. Truly a beast of the fire and the flame!

LONG-NECKS AND SEA LIZARDS

There are several exceedingly mysterious creatures that are distinctly dragonesque in appearance, and, although they have been recorded, many are still unidentified and unaccepted by science.

Two of the most striking and potentially sensational are the long-neck and the sea lizard. Some unidentified lake monsters and sea serpents have a long, erect neck and a proportionately small head, whose silhouette is frequently likened by eyewitnesses to that of a periscope.

The most famous representative of these is a shy lake-dweller from Scotland—the Loch Ness monster. Numerous "periscope" sightings of what appears to be a long-necked mystery animal swimming in the loch have been reported over the years, particularly since a new lochside road was built in 1933.

It is less well known, however, that a few people claim to have spied "Nessie" moving or resting on land. These accounts afford an insight into the physical characteristics of the entire animal, not just its head, neck, and back. From such descriptions, Nessie is roughly 30 feet (9 m) long, with a robust body possessing two pairs of paddle-shaped limbs and a long pointed tail, as well as a long neck and small head.

No modern-day animal fits this description; but there is a family of creatures from prehistoric times that corresponds precisely with it, the

plesiosaurs—swan-necked, flippered, fish-eating aquatic reptiles. There were many different species of plesiosaur, but the last seemingly died out with the dinosaurs some 65 million years ago. There is still no satisfactory explanation for their demise, since they appear to have been highly successful and able to withstand competition from

As this illustration conveys, the boundary between long-necks and sea lizards and fictional aquatic dragons is tenuous.

Another perplexing category of water monster can be dubbed the sea lizard, because accounts of such beasts conjure up images of immense, water-dwelling lizards, with crocodilian heads and a ferocious mien worthy of the most dreadful dragon.

On July 30, 1915, during World War I, a German submarine, the U-28, torpedoed the British steamer *Iberian* near the Fastnet Rock, off Ireland; but less than a minute after the ship had sunk, a huge underwater explosion blasted a gigantic, writhing monster out of the sea. According to the account later given by the captain of the U-28, it was about 60 feet (18 m) long and shaped like a crocodile, with a long pointed tail and four limbs with powerful webbed feet. It fell back into the sea a few moments later and disappeared without trace.

In some reports, the sea lizard's limbs are likened to flippers rather than webbed feet, but otherwise there is little difference between them. Three separate types of animal fit this description, but again they were all believed to have become extinct with or before the dinosaurs.

One is the pliosaur—a type of plesiosaur with a shorter neck than the familiar version, but with a much larger and longer head and massive jaws like an alligator. The second candidate is the mosasaur—a true sea lizard, related to today's monitors, yet specialized for an aquatic existence, with a flattened, finned tail, flippers, and a crocodilian head. The third is the thalattosuchian—a highly evolved marine crocodile, with a slender streamlined body, flippered limbs, and a dorsal fin on its long tail. If any of these creatures has modern-day survivors evading scientific detection, the sea lizard's identity would be a mystery no longer.

other aquatic predators. So perhaps they did not die out, but are sufficiently elusive to avoid close contact with man. Such a theory may seem radical, but it could explain the plethora of reports from many parts of the world concerning mystifying freshwater and marine beasts that bear an uncanny resemblance to living plesiosaurs.

DRAGONS OF THE FUTURE

We need not mourn too morosely the dragons of the past, nor need we look with disappointed eyes on their zoologically uninspiring namesakes of the present.

For there are still bona fide, corporeal dragons, such as the long-neck, sea lizard, serpent whale, *artrellia*, *inkhomi*, tatzelworm, and others of their cryptic kind to torment and tantalize the staid world of traditional zoology. And these creatures of controversy offer good reason indeed for believing that the future still holds many great surprises and joys in store for the dedicated dracontologist.

Similarly, far from diminishing in appeal as an irrelevant anachronism with the rapid approach of the ultra-scientific twenty-first century, the image of the dragon is experiencing a profound upsurge in international popularity that no human superstar could ever emulate. Today it is stunningly evoked and harnessed by modern technology for every conceivable purpose, including films, the toy and fashion industries, CD-ROM, and promotional publicity campaigns of breathtaking artistic splendor.

It seems certain, therefore, (St. George notwithstanding) that the dragon—the embodiment of dynamic, uncompromising, irresistible power—will continue to evolve, diversify, and populate our planet for a long time to come.

The dragon is dead—long live the dragon!

A late 20th-century dragon: this spectacular poster advertises Pirelli's "Dragon GT" motorcycle tires.

BIBLIOGRAPHY

There is insufficient space to list the numerous articles on dragons and the many general works consulted during the preparation of this volume, but the specialized books listed below are recommended to the reader for further reference.

Allen, Judy and **Jeanne Griffiths** *The Book of the Dragon* Orbis, London, 1979

Ashton, John *Curious Creatures in Zoology* John C. Nimmo, London, 1980

Barber, Richard and **Anne Riches** *A Dictionary of Fabulous Beasts* Macmillan, London, 1971

Barrett, Charles *The Bunyip and Other Mythical Monsters and Legends* Mail Newspapers, Melbourne, 1946

Binyon, Laurence *The Flight of the Dragon* John Murray, London, 1911

Borges, Jorge L. *The Book of Imaginary Beings* Penguin Books, Harmondsworth (rev.), 1974

Bose, Hampden C. du *The Dragon, Image and Demon* Presbyterian Committee of Publications, Richmond, 1899

Burland, C. and **W. Froman** *Feathered Serpent and Smoking Mirror* Orbis, London, 1975

Byrne, M. St. Clare (ed.) *The Elizabethan Zoo* Frederick Etchells & Hugh MacDonald, London, 1926

Campbell, John F. *The Celtic Dragon Myth* John Grant, Edinburgh, 1911

Carrington, Richard *Mermaids and Mastodons: A Book of Natural and Unnatural History* Chatto & Windus, London, 1957

Carter, Frederick *The Dragon of the Alchemists* E. Matthews, London, 1926

Clair, Colin *Unnatural History: An Illustrated Bestiary* Abelard-Schuman, London, 1967

Clark, Anne *Beasts and Bawdy* J.M. Dent, London, 1975

Cohen, Daniel *A Modern Look at Monsters* Tower Publications, New York, 1970

———— *The Encyclopedia of Monsters* Dodd, Mead & Co., New York, 1982

Coleman, Loren *Curious Encounters* Faber & Faber, London, 1985

Cooper, J.C. *Symbolic and Mythological Animals* Aquarian Press, London, 1992

Cooper, William R. *Serpent Myths of Ancient Egypt* Robert Hardwicke, London, 1873

Costello, Peter *The Magic Zoo: The Natural History of Fabulous Animals* Sphere Books, London, 1979

Dance, S. Peter *Animal Fakes and Frauds* Sampson Low, Maidenhead, 1976

Dickinson, Peter *The Flight of Dragons* Pierrot Publishing, London, 1979

Dimmick, Adrian N. *Worme Worlde: The Dragon Trivia Source Book* The Dragon Trust, London, 1994

Dinsdale, Tim *The Leviathans* Futura, London (rev.), 1976

Elliot-Smith, Grafton *The Evolution of the Dragon* University Press, Manchester, 1919

Epstein, Perle *Monsters: Their Histories, Homes, and Habits* Doubleday, Garden City, 1973

Farson, Daniel and **Angus Hall** *Mysterious Monsters* Aldus Books, London, 1978

Fox, David S. *Saint George: The Saint With Three Faces* Kensal Press, Shooter's Lodge, 1983

Frazer, James G. *The Golden Bough: A Study in Magic and Religion* Macmillan, London (3rd ed.), 1911–15

Gifford, Douglas and **John Sibbick** *Warriors, Gods and Spirits From Central and South American Mythology* Peter Lowe, Wallingford, 1983

Gould, Charles *Mythical Monsters* W.H. Allen, London, 1886

———— with **Malcolm Smith** (ed.) *The Dragon* Wildwood House, London, 1977

Green, Roger L. (ed.) *A Cavalcade of Dragons* H.Z. Walck, New York, 1970

Gubernatis, Angelo de *Zoological Mythology: The Legends of Animals* Trübner, London, 1872

Guirand, Felix (ed.) *New Larousse Encyclopedia of Mythology* Hamlyn, London, 1968

Hall, Mark A. *Thunderbirds! The Living Legend of Giant Birds* Mark A. Hall Publications and Research, Bloomington, 1988

Hargreaves, Joyce *The Dragon Hunter's Handbook* Granada, London, 1983

———— *Hargreaves New Illustrated Bestiary* Gothic Image, Glastonbury, 1990

Hayes, L. Newton *The Chinese Dragon* Commercial Press, Shanghai, 1922

Headon, Deidre *Mythical Beasts* Hutchinson, London, 1981

Heuvelmans, Bernard *On the Track of Unknown Animals* Rupert Hart-Davis, London, 1958
———— *In the Wake of the Sea-Serpents* Rupert Hart-Davis, London, 1965
———— *Les Derniers Dragons d'Afrique* Plon, Paris, 1978
Hogarth, P. and **V. Clery** *Dragons* Allen Lane, London, 1979
Hoke, Helen (ed.) *Dragons, Dragons, Dragons* Franklin Watts, New York, 1972
Holiday, F.W. *The Dragon and the Disc* Sidgwick & Jackson, London, 1973
Holman, Felice and **Nanine Valen** *The Drac: French Tales of Dragons and Demons* Charles Scribner's Sons, New York, 1975
Hoult, Janet *Dragons: Their History and Symbolism* Gothic Image, Glastonbury, 1987
Hulme, F. Edward *Natural History Lore and Legend* Bernard Quaritch, London, 1895
Huxley, Francis *The Dragon: Nature of Spirit, Spirit of Nature* Thames and Hudson, London, 1979
Ingersoll, Ernest *Dragons and Dragon Lore* Payson & Clarke, New York, 1928
Johnsgard, Paul and **Karin** *Dragons and Unicorns: A Natural History* St. Martin's Press, New York, 1982
Journal of the Dragon Trust, Nos. 1–4, *The Dragon Chronicle*, 1994 and 1995
Lehner, E. and **J.** *A Fantastic Bestiary* Tudor, New York, 1969
Ley, Willy *The Lungfish and the Unicorn* Modern Age, New York, 1941
———— *Exotic Zoology* Viking, New York, 1959
Lum, Peter *Fabulous Beasts* Thames and Hudson, London, 1952
Mackal, Roy P. *A Living Dinosaur? In Search of Mokele-Mbembe* E.J. Brill, Leiden, 1987
Mackenzie, D.A. *Myths and Legends of China and Japan* Gresholm Publishing, London, 1923
Meurger, M. and **C. Gagnon** *Lake Monster Traditions: A Cross-Cultural Analysis* Fortean Tomes, London, 1988
Miller, C. *A Dictionary of Monsters and Mysterious Beasts* Piccolo, London, 1974
Morris, Ramona and **Desmond** *Men and Snakes* Hutchinson, London, 1965

Newman, Paul *The Hill of the Dragon: An Enquiry into the Nature of Dragon Legends* Rowman & Littlefield, Totowa, 1980
Phillips, Henry *Basilisks and Cockatrices* E. Stern, Philadelphia, 1882
Robinson, Margaret W. *Fictitious Beasts: A Bibliography* The Library Association, London, 1961
Rovin, J. *The Encyclopedia of Monsters* Facts on File, Oxford, 1989
Rudd, Elizabeth (ed.) *Dragons* W.H. Allen, London, 1980
Sanders, Tao Tao Liu *Dragons, Gods and Spirits From Chinese Mythology* Schocken Books, New York, 1983
Screeton, Paul *The Lambton Worm and Other Northumbrian Dragon Legends* Zodiac House, Fulham, 1978
Shuker, Karl P.N. *Extraordinary Animals Worldwide* Robert Hale, London, 1991
———— *The Lost Ark: New and Rediscovered Animals of the 20th Century* HarperCollins, London, 1993
———— *In Search of Prehistoric Survivors* Blandford, London, 1995
———— (consultant) *Man and Beast; Secrets of the Natural World* Reader's Digest, Pleasantville, 1993
Simpson, J. *British Dragons* B.T. Batsford, London, 1980
South, Malcolm (ed.) *Topsell's Histories of Beasts* Nelson-Hall, Chicago, 1981
Spicer, Dorothy G. *13 Dragons* Coward, McCann & Geoghegan, New York, 1974

Time-Life Books *The Enchanted World: Dragons* Amsterdam, 1984
———— *The Enchanted World: Magical Beasts* Amsterdam, 1985
Trevelyan, M. *Folklore and Folk-Stories of Wales* Elliot Stock, London, 1909
Trubshaw, Bob *Dragon Slaying Myths Ancient and Modern* Heart of Albion Press, Wymeswold, 1993
Vinycomb, John *Fictitious and Symbolic Creatures in Art* Chapman & Hall, London, 1906
Visser, Marinus W. de *The Dragon in China and Japan* Johannes Müller, Amsterdam, 1858
White, T.H. *The Book of Beasts* Jonathan Cape, London, 1954
Whitlock, Ralph *Here Be Dragons* George Allen & Unwin, London, 1983
Wignell, Edel (ed.) *A Boggle of Bunyips* Hodder & Stoughton, Sydney, 1981

A Russian icon, painted on a wooden panel c.1600, shows St. George destroying a very serpentine dragon.

INDEX

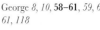

Acknowledgments

Picture credits
t = top; *b* = bottom

Endpapers Fortean Picture Library; **1** Images Colour Library; **2–3** Lambeth Palace Library, London/The Bridgeman Art Library; **4–5** Jean-Loup Charmet; **8** AKG London; **9** Jean-Loup Charmet; **10** National Gallery, London/The Bridgeman Art Library; **11** Garland Picture Library; **12** Fortean Picture Library; **14** Leslie Garland Picture Library; **15** Mary Evans Picture Library; **16–17** The Fotomas Index; **18** Robert Francis/Robert Harding Picture Library; **19** Adam Woolfitt/Robert Harding Picture Library; **20** Jean-Louis Charmet; **21** AKG London; **22** Werner Forman Archive; **23** Stofnun Arna Magnússonar; **28–29t** Mary Evans Picture Library; **29b** Gunther Ziesler/Bruce Coleman Ltd.; **30–31** Scala; **32** Museo Nazionale, Taranto/The Bridgeman Art Library; **33–36** Mary Evans Picture Library; **37** Fitzwilliam Museum, University of Cambridge/The Bridgeman Art Library; **39** John Lucas Scudamore Coll./The Bridgeman Art Library; **41–42** Images Colour Library; **43** Mary Evans Picture Library; **45** AKG London; **46** British Film Institute; **47** Werner Forman Archive; **48** Hulton Deutsch Collection; **49** Musée Condé, Chantilly/Giraudon/The Bridgeman Art Library; **51** Images Colour Library; **52–53** Mary Evans Picture Library; **54** Louvre, Paris/The Bridgeman Art Library; **55** The British Museum; **56** Mary Evans Picture Library; **57** Jean-Loup Charmet; **58–59** Scuola di San Giorgio degli Schiavoni, Venice/The Bridgeman

Art Library; **60** Victoria & Albert Museum/Michael Holford; **61** E.T. Archive; **63–68** Fortean Picture Library; **69** Jean-Loup Charmet; **70–71** State Museum, Berlin/Werner Forman Archive; **72** Professor Roy Mackal; **73** Mary Evans Picture Library; **75** Ann Ronan at Picture Select; **76** Bruce Coleman Ltd.; **77** Mary Evans Picture Library; **78–79** Essex Record Office; **81** Valley of the Queens, Thebes, Egypt/The Bridgeman Art Library; **82–83** Werner Forman Archive; **84** Mireille Vautier; **86–87** AKG London; **88** Images Colour Library; **89** Hulton Deutsch Collection; **91** Jean-Loup Charmet; **93** Private Collection/The Bridgeman Art Library; **97** The Fotomas Index; **98t** Bibliothèque Nationale; **98b** Dr. Karl P.N. Shuker/ Fortean Picture Library; **100–101** Réunion des Musées Nationaux/ Duplicata; **102** Saint-Sauveur Cathedral, Aix-en-Provence/Giraudon/The Bridgeman Art Library; **103** Mary Evans Picture Library; **106** Reinaldo Viegas/Calouste Gulbenkian Foundation; **107** Mary Evans Picture Library; **108** Jean-Loup Charmet; **109** Scala; **110–111** Charmet/Mary Evans Picture Library; **112** Fortean Picture Library; **113** Dr. Eckart Pott/Bruce Coleman Ltd.; **114–115** Trevor Beer; **116** CPK Auto Products Ltd.; **117** Jean-Loup Charmet; **118** AKG London; **119–120** Jean-Loup Charmet

Artwork credits
Lorraine Harrison (map) 6–7
Janetta Turgle (line) 24–25, 104–5
Helena Zakrzewska-Rucinska (color) 13, 16–17, 24–25, 26–27, 62–63, 66–67, 75, 78–79, 95, 97, 98b, 99, 104–5, 114–15